Once Upon a Miracle

Dramas for Worship and Religious Education

by
Michael E. Moynahan, S.J.

5-14-93

Phil,

Here's to the miracle of creativity.
Bring it to all you do at Regis.

Ad multos annos.

XXoo,

Moyna

PAULIST PRESS
New York/Mahwah, N.J.

Library of Congress Cataloging-in-Publication Data

Moynahan, Michael E.
    Once upon a miracle : dramas for worship and religious education /
  by Michael E. Moynahan.
      p. cm.
    ISBN 0-8091-3361-X (pbk.)
    1. Drama in Christian education.   2. Drama in public worship.
  3. Catholic Church—Education.   4. Catholic Church—Liturgy.
  5. Bible plays, American.   I. Title.
  BV1534.4.M68   1993
  246′.7—dc20   92-41325
                                                                    CIP

Published by Paulist Press
997 Macarthur Boulevard
Mahwah, NJ 07430

Printed and bound in the
United States of America

Contents

*This book is dedicated
to the Biblical Explorers,
past, present,
and still to come.*

Introduction

In September of 1983, I left the Jesuit School of Theology in Berkeley, California. During my years of graduate study and teaching at the Graduate Theological Union, I was able to form the Berkeley Liturgical Drama Guild and create, through the shared faith and religious imagination of its members, over thirty-five dramatizations and mimes based on biblical stories. It was a wonderfully creative and rewarding time in my life.

For two years (1983–1985), I enjoyed the hospitality of Fr. Anthony Sauer[1] and the St. Ignatius Community in San Francisco, California, during the intervals of my travels throughout Australia, the Pacific and different parts of the United States and Canada offering short courses and workshops on the potential uses of drama in worship and religious education. During those two years of extensive travel I became acutely aware that I had stopped producing any new creative drama based on biblical material. There were a number of reasons for this.

The biblical dramatizations in *How The Word Became Flesh*[2] and *Once Upon a Parable*[3] were all attempts to give artistic expression to the shared faith of a community. The Berkeley Liturgical Drama Guild had been a microcosm of the Graduate Theological Union community. Its members came from the different GTU schools. I no longer had that community, and my traveling and extensive workshop commitments precluded the possibility of becoming a part of such a nurturing and challenging faith community.

Toward the end of my second year of traveling and speaking, I knew that I needed a more permanent faith community if I were to create any further biblical dramatizations. I explained this to a very understanding and supportive religious superior of mine (Paul Belcher, S.J.)[4] who immediately began work on a possible appointment at Santa Clara University. In September of

1

1985 I joined the Campus Ministry Staff at Santa Clara and began teaching part time in the Religious Studies Department.

I went to Santa Clara with a number of fears and concerns. In Berkeley I had worked with adults who brought a wealth of experience to our shared-faith process. I would now be working with young adults. Would there be enough experience or faith to continue this biblical drama process? While our first steps were small and halting, the answer was a resounding "Yes!" The work of the Berkeley Liturgical Drama Guild has been continued and furthered through the efforts of Biblical Explorers, a group of university staff and students who faithfully meet each Sunday evening for ninety minutes to explore together the riches of biblical material.

Increasingly I am convinced that scripture should be studied and faith shared together. Different eyes, different minds and different hearts find different treasures buried deep in the biblical material. No one of us can completely uncover all the riches that the scriptures have to offer us. Especially when we find ourselves in some of life's more puzzling and confusing periods, we need what other people see and hear that we are simply blind and deaf to. Just as we need what they see and hear during our times of blindness and deafness, they will need our eyes and ears and understanding hearts at other times.

The other concern that I had was whether Campus Ministry and the Santa Clara University community would be open to a group sharing its faith through an occasional biblical drama within the context of worship. Fr. Dan Germann, Director of Campus Ministry when I first came to Santa Clara University, and his successor, Sister Maureen Schaukowitch, were wonderfully supportive and encouraging of this creative faith venture.

The students who have joined the Biblical Explorers over the past six years, as well as the students who have been touched in a hundred different ways by the biblical dramatizations we have shared in the Mission Church on the campus, are living testimony to the validity of this creative faith adventure and the vitality of the "Good News" in our society and culture when we communicate it in a language people can comprehend. The challenge before us now was wonderfully articulated in the document *Fulfilled in Your Hearing: The Homily in the Sunday Assembly*.[5]

The challenge this document presents to all those who study the scriptures, and particularly those who would preach on them, is to constantly make *connections* between the reality of the scriptures and the reality of our lived experience. In this way, life becomes an interpretive tool for understanding the meaning of scripture. Conversely, scripture becomes an important interpretive tool and a light that can reveal the genuine meaning of our life experience today. For people of faith, these are two indispensable tools. And we dare not lose touch with either or we risk twisting and distorting both the scriptures and our experience.

The miracle stories in the New Testament presented us with a number of unexpected challenges. Miracle stories generally are more dramatic in nature than their parable counterparts. The action of the miracle stories (e.g., *The Raising of Lazarus* or *The Healing of the Gerasene Demoniac*) tends to be much more dramatic than that found in many of the parables that Jesus told (e.g., *The Mustard Seed, The Pearl, The Publican and Pharisee*) although there would be some notable exceptions to this. The challenge, apart from trying to understand the miracle stories, was how to dramatize already dramatic stories.

We once again drew upon the *Key Word Process* that I discussed in *Once Upon a Parable*.[6] Since stories and dramas unfold through actions, the Biblical Explorers examined the miracle stories paying particular attention to the *verbs* or *actions* of the story. The shape that our understanding or interpretation took, however, was not an entirely new story based on the original one. The final form of the dramas consisted in three or four dramatic vignettes which were woven together by some theme or haunting biblical refrain. Most of the dramas in *Once Upon a Miracle* resemble more the overhead stage lights of a theatrical production which illumine now one area of dramatic action on the stage, and then another.

These biblical dramas do not and will not replace the scriptural stories they are imaginatively and dramatically interpreting. They are the attempt of one faith community to understand and release the transforming power of the "Good News" that is the gospel. They are the attempt of one faith community to put into practice Heinrich Zimmer's advice about sacred texts: "They are the everlasting oracles of life. They have to be questioned and consulted anew, with every age, each approaching them with its own inevitable questions. . . . The replies already given, therefore, cannot be made to serve us. The powers have to be consulted again directly—again, again, and again. Our primary task is to learn not so much what they are said to have said, as how to approach them, evoke fresh speech from them, and understand that speech."[7]

In Biblical Explorers, the tools that allowed us to approach these sacred texts (i.e., scriptural stories), evoke fresh speech from them and understand that speech, were shared faith, creativity, imagination and drama. *Once Upon a Miracle* invites you, your Bible study or faith-sharing group, your class or parish liturgy group to bring those same gifts and tools to your experience and exploration of these scriptural stories and biblical dramas. If you do and when you do, they will nurture you, challenge you and change you. The scriptures will, the dramas will, and the study questions and exercises will, if you let them. They continually did this for the Biblical Explorers, and I am confident they will do the same for you and the group with which you work.

How should you use the material in *Once Upon a Miracle*? I believe you can do this in a variety of ways. The story dramatizations, as well as the reflection questions and exercises, can be used for your own personal faith enrichment. If you are part of a liturgy coordinating group, the biblical dramas, or at least some parts of them, might be rehearsed and used by your group as a dramatized homily at a liturgy on some special occasion. And finally, if you are part of a Bible study group, or if you are a teacher of religious education, the scriptures, the biblical dramatizations, the reflection questions and exercises can offer you a wealth of material for your class or group to explore. Please don't allow any of the material in this book to become a straightjacket. Use the vignettes in each drama and the particular study questions and exercises which follow each drama that will best address your experiences and your needs.

The format for each of the nine biblical dramatizations is the same. First, you will see the original biblical story. Second, you will have the biblical dramatization created by the Biblical Explorers. Following each dramatization will be the *Props* list we used in our production of the dramatization and some *Produc-*

tion Notes which give you some understanding of the occasion, the congregation and circumstances that helped shape our understanding and interpretation of each biblical story with which we worked. Third, you will find eight (8) reflection questions and exercises based upon the particular scriptural story and particular biblical dramatization you are exploring.

Finally, some thanks are in order. I am grateful to Larry Boadt, my editor at Paulist Press, for his encouragement of this project. I am grateful to John Privett, S.J.,[8] and the Jesuit Community of Santa Clara University, for giving me the time and opportunity to fashion these biblical dramatizations into a spiritual and catechetical tool. I am grateful to the Jesuit community of Farm Street Church in London for offering me a place to work. The environment they provided me was both challenging, stimulating and rewarding. I am grateful to the Campus Ministry team at Santa Clara University for their continued support and encouragement of Biblical Explorers. And I am most grateful to those people at Santa Clara University who have explored and shared the riches of scripture with me: Krysha Cox, Rosemary O'Brien, Garth Ashbeck, Michele Anselmo, Pam Romano, David Giammona, Michael Gilson, Anne Ensminger, Craig De Pole, Frances Ambrose, Cari Zieske, Joe Montes, Christi Montes, John Cottrell, Jenny Girard, Jim Quaranta, Brian Bogucki, Larry Daquino, Gregg Servis, Tarie Regan, Kevin Van Slambrook, Eric Steuben, Chris Fowler, Carolyn Otis, Ignacio Osorio, Tricia Keady, Todd Gardiner, Brenda Modkins, Paul Leonard, Brian Ching, Laura Nichols, Lisa Wang, Duchess Lacap, Laura Bertone, Krista Hein, Dan McKenzie, Anne Sullivan, Ron Andre, Marcy Miller, Brennan Swanberg, Alison Laventhol, Mark Lang, Kristie Schindele, Jeff McCabe, Eric Loo, Jen Elmore, Marco Campagna, Susan Deax, Peter Lampe, Brian Hickey, Nancy Nissen, Lelanya Black, Sean Murphy, Bro. Ben Foy, and many more whose names are lodged behind some rusty synapse in my brain. You all have a permanent place in my grateful Irish heart.

Biblical Explorers has been nurtured and built upon the faith of those who have gone before us. May all of you who enter into these biblical explorations with faith and imagination realize that others will come who will build upon all you uncover and share. May our faith, then, continue to be shared. May the riches of the scriptures continue to be explored. May the power of the "Good News" continue to find ever-fresh and imaginative expression as we are molded into new and vital stories of the miraculous presence of God's love in our world.

NOTES

1. During these two years, Fr. Tony Sauer was the religious superior of the Jesuit Community at St. Ignatius College Preparatory. Currently he is president of the same school.
2. Michael E. Moynahan, S.J., *How The Word Became Flesh* (San Jose: Resource Publications, 1979).
3. Michael E. Moynahan, S.J., *Once Upon a Parable* (New York: Paulist Press, 1984).
4. Currently Provincial of the Jesuits in the California Province of the Society of Jesus. In 1985 he was the Provincial Assistant for Education.
5. The Bishops' Committee on Priestly Life and Ministry, *Fulfilled in Your Hearing: The Homily in the Sunday Assembly* (Washington, D.C.: United States Catholic Conference, 1982).
6. *Once Upon a Parable,* pp. 6–7.
7. Heinrich Zimmer, *The King and the Corpse,* edited by Joseph Campbell (Princeton: Princeton University Press, 1957), p. 4.
8. Religious superior of the Jesuit Community at Santa Clara University.

1. The Raising of Lazarus

(John 11:1–44)

Now a certain man was ill, Lazarus of Bethany, the village of Mary and her sister Martha. It was Mary who anointed the Lord with ointment and wiped his feet with her hair, whose brother Lazarus was ill. So the sisters sent to him, saying, "Lord, he whom you love is ill." But when Jesus heard it he said, "This illness is not unto death; it is for the glory of God, so that the Son of God may be glorified by means of it."

Now Jesus loved Martha and her sister and Lazarus.

So when he heard that he was ill, he stayed two days longer in the place where he was. Then after this he said to the disciples, "Let us go into Judea again." The disciples said to him, "Rabbi, the Jews were but now seeking to stone you, and are you going there again?" Jesus answered, "Are there not twelve hours in the day? If any one walks in the day, he does not stumble, because he sees the light of this world. But if any one walks in the night, he stumbles, because the light is not in him." Thus he spoke, and then he said to them, "Our friend Lazarus has fallen asleep, but I go to awaken him out of sleep." The disciples said to him, "Lord, if he has fallen asleep, he will recover." Now Jesus had spoken of his death, but they thought that he meant taking rest in sleep. Then Jesus told them plainly, "Lazarus is dead; and for your sake I am glad that I was not there, so that you may believe. But let us go to him." Thomas, called the Twin, said to his fellow disciples, "Let us also go, that we may die with him."

Now when Jesus came, he found that Lazarus had already been in the tomb four days. Bethany was near Jerusalem, about two miles off, and many of the Jews had come to Martha and Mary to console them concerning their brother. When Martha heard that Jesus was coming, she went and met him, while Mary sat in the house. Martha said to Jesus, "Lord, if you had been here, my brother would not have died. And even now I know that whatever you ask from God, God will give you." Jesus said to her, "Your brother will rise again." Martha said to him, "I know that he will rise again in the resurrection at the last day." Jesus said to her, "I am the resurrection and the life; he who believes in me, though he die, yet shall he live, and whoever lives and believes in me shall never die. Do you believe this?" She said to him, "Yes, Lord; I believe that you are the Christ, the Son of God, he who is coming into the world."

When she had said this, she went and called her sister Mary, saying quietly, "The Teacher is here and is calling for you." And when she heard it, she rose quickly and went to him. Now Jesus had not yet come to the village, but was still in the place where Martha had met him. When the Jews who were with her in the house, consoling her, saw Mary rise quickly and go out, they followed her, supposing that she was going to the tomb to weep there. Then Mary, when she came where Jesus was and saw him, fell at this feet, saying to him, "Lord, if you had been here, my brother would not have died." When Jesus saw her weeping, and the Jews who came with her also weeping, he was deeply moved in spirit and troubled; and he said, "Where have you laid him?" They said to him, "Lord, come and see." Jesus wept. So the Jews said, "See how he loved him!" But some of them said, "Could not he who opened the eyes of the blind man have kept this man from dying?"

Then Jesus, deeply moved again, came to the tomb; it was a cave, and a stone lay upon it. Jesus said, "Take away the stone." Martha, the sister of the dead man, said to him, "Lord, by this time there will be an odor, for he has been dead four days." Jesus said to her, "Did I not tell you that if you would believe you would see the glory of God?" So they took away the stone. And Jesus lifted up his eyes and said, "Father, I thank thee that thou hast heard me. I knew that thou hearest me always, but I have said this on account of the people standing by, that they may believe that thou didst send me." When he had said this, he cried with a loud voice, "Lazarus, come out." The dead man came out, his hands and feet bound with bandages, and his face wrapped with a cloth. Jesus said to them, "Unbind him, and let him go."

The Raising of Lazarus

CAST

Jesus	Critic
Disciple-1	Placard Bearer
Disciple-2	Tempter-1
Messenger	Tempter-2
Martha	Tempter-3
Mary	Spirit
Lazarus	

[**Note:** The entire first part of this dramatization is mimed with music. It should have the broadness of a melodrama as well as a silent movie effect. Placards are used to indicate the action or passage of time. The second part of the dramatization is of a more serious nature and will involve, basically, Jesus, the Spirit of Jesus, Lazarus, and three Temptations of Lazarus (personified). The second part of the dramatization will utilize mime and dialogue.]

PART ONE

[*Actions are extremely stylized for a humorous effect. Play this part of the drama like* The King of Kings *or* The Ten Commandments *(silent movie classics by Cecil B. De Mille).*]

1. After the proclamation of the Word (Jn 11:1–44), all sit. Music begins (I suggest the opening four or five minutes of Beetho-

ven's Fifth Symphony) as a placard is brought out to center stage (sanctuary or acting area) which reads: *RAISING OF LAZARUS.*

2. When this placard is taken away, another is brought in which reads: *THE BAD NEWS.* In this scene, Jesus is stoically addressing his disciples when someone rushes in with the horrible news. The messenger gestures how Jesus' good friend Lazarus is dying. The messenger does this with three gestural movements: (a) pointing a strong finger at Jesus, (b) strongly clasping and bringing both hands over his heart, and (c) using his right forefinger like a knife and drawing it across his throat. Jesus, impassive, sends the bewildered messenger away. The disciples look at him in wide-eyed horror.

3. The third placard is brought on which reads: *LAZARUS DIES.* The character Lazarus can come on and have a lengthy melodramatic death scene depicting the illness and reaching out for help. The placard bearer finally hits Lazarus over the head with a clown hammer or the placard and Lazarus dies.

4. The fourth placard is brought on which reads: *JESUS MEETS MARTHA.* In this scene, Martha comes up and ventilates her anger at Jesus for not coming sooner. No words are used. This is all mimed and gestured exaggeratedly. Extensive use of the face should be used. Finally, Jesus puts up his hands signifying "That's Enough!" and directs her to go home. She leaves, bewildered. The disciples are shocked.

5. The fifth placard is brought on which reads: *JESUS MEETS MARY.* Mary comes in from a distance weeping copious tears. She keeps throwing toilet paper or tissues to her right, her left, in front of her and behind her. Jesus is visibly bothered by Mary's crying. The disciples try to discreetly tell her to stop. Mary doesn't notice them and her grieving becomes more intense. Finally, Jesus, gesturing his frustration, reaches out and chokes Mary. She stops crying and looks bewildered. Jesus gestures her to go home.

6. The sixth card is brought on which reads: *JESUS DOES HIS STUFF.* Here Jesus walks to the area where Lazarus is lying. Jesus instructs the disciples to get back and give him some room. They ignore his instructions and Jesus finally has to personally place them at a safe distance. Jesus then goes back to Lazarus, takes off his watch, rolls up his sleeves and raises his arms to heaven. He immediately receives electricity (symbolizing power) and is shaking all over. Finally, Jesus directs one hand in the direction of Lazarus who begins to quicken. Lazarus shakes more and more back to life. When Lazarus is standing, he moves toward Jesus with open arms as Jesus moves toward Lazarus with open arms. They pass and look back bewildered. They turn and try again, missing once again. The third time, with the help of a few head fakes, they finally meet and embrace.

7. All the characters come together and begin taking a couple of bows. The audience begins to applaud. Someone in the congregation stands up and speaks. This begins the second part of the drama. This person is an interrupter.

PART TWO

CRITIC:
　　You mean that is it? There is nothing more?

JESUS:
　　What do you mean?

CRITIC:
　　I mean, you'll have to do better than that.

LAZARUS:
　　What are you talking about?

CRITIC:
　　I can turn on Walt Disney's "Wonderful World of Color" and see what you've just done!

PLACARD:

What's wrong with what we've just done?

CRITIC:

It's too simple. It's too black and white. Where are all those annoying gray areas? Your story is too neat and clean. Our living is messy. Our dying is messy.

JESUS:

Then get a maid.

CRITIC:

Your "Raising of Lazarus" was just too easy, too nice, too predictable, too romantic. It was unreal. Where's the mess? If this is supposed to be "Good News" then how does it speak to our mess?

MARTHA:

Well, if you think you can do better, why don't you come up here and try it yourself.

MARY:

Yeah. We worked for weeks on this, wise guy! (*The Critic goes up and huddles briefly with the players. Fragmentary comments are heard such as: "What a waste of time!" "Are you kidding?" "That'll never work!" "Hey, give him a chance!" The Critic begins to position the players.*)

CRITIC:

Try it this way. We are at the tomb. The scene focuses on Jesus and his good friend Lazarus who has just died. Jesus, accompanied by friends, goes to the tomb. After weeping for God only knows what, Jesus calls out to his friend. And here the scene begins. For why should Lazarus come out of the tomb, that protective womb of security? (*The Critic sits down and the action continues after a few moments of silence. Lazarus is positioned in the tomb (UL). The three Tempters position themselves behind Lazarus. Jesus (DRC) has his Spirit crouched down in front of him. A few of the disciples are behind Jesus (DR) at a distance. When everyone is in place Jesus begins.*)

JESUS:

Lazarus, come forth! (*Here the Spirit of Jesus goes toward Lazarus in swirling motions, i.e., circles, toward the entrance to the tomb. The Spirit then gestures by reaching out her left hand toward Lazarus. When Lazarus is stopped by one of the Tempters, the Spirit falls to the floor. When Lazarus finally makes his way to Jesus, the Spirit leads him.*)

LAZARUS:

Huhhhhh? (*Lazarus quickens and groans. It is as if he is just waking up. He starts to move toward the entrance to the tomb when Tempter-1 comes forward.*)

TEMPTER-1:

Where do you think you're going?

LAZARUS:

Outside.

TEMPTER-1:

You can't go out there.

LAZARUS:

Why not?

TEMPTER-1:

Because you stink! You smell of death! Look at you! Your hair is falling out. You're not getting any younger, you know! Look, maybe this wasn't the best possible death, but at least it's over. Isn't one lifetime of pain and sorrow enough? Do you want to go through all that confusion and uncertainty again? That being suspended in midair somewhere between knowing and not knowing? You've experienced one lifetime of disappointments and failures. Face the facts. Was life all that great? Why do you want to put yourself through all of that again?

JESUS:

Lazarus, come forth! (*The Spirit again extends a hand in invitation to Lazarus. Lazarus looks from Tempter-1 back in the direction of Jesus and begins to take another step toward Jesus when Tempter-2 speaks up.*)

TEMPTER-2:

Not so fast, Laz! Think for a moment about what's going to happen when you go out there. What are you going to meet? Don't you think you might have a little believability problem? It's called the "Credibility Gap." And that's you, Lazarus! First you're declared dead. Now you're declared living. Well, which is it? Are you dead or alive? Who will be able to believe you anymore? You'll be a walking paradox. You can't go out there. You're too incredible!

JESUS:

Lazarus, come forth! (*The Spirit once again extends a hand in invitation to Lazarus. He looks from Tempter-2 back to the direction of Jesus. He takes a breath and starts to take another step in the direction of Jesus. Just then Tempter-3 steps forward.*)

TEMPTER-3:

Slow down, buddy, you're moving too fast. Do you really want to do this? (*Lazarus nods his head indicating "yes."*) But what for? (*Lazarus simply points to Jesus.*) Him? Look at it this way, pal. Why do you think he's doing this? For you? Don't kid yourself! This so-called friend of yours is not doing this for you. Jesus is doing this for himself. Good old Lazarus, taken to the cleaners again! When will you learn? Where was he three days ago when you really needed him? Listen, buster, he's just using you to showcase his power! And if he'd do this to you, and he's supposed to be your best friend, imagine what those other idiots out there will do to you. Why they'll con you to death. In no time at all you'll find yourself right back here! So look at it this way: you were alone out there and you're alone in here. What's the difference? At least here you won't be bothered. Here you can rest in peace!

JESUS:

> Lazarus, come forth! (*The Spirit gestures to Lazarus again. He slowly begins to take another step towards Jesus when all three Tempters verbally bombard him.*)

TEMPTER-1:

> Well, it looks like you're not going to take our advice.

TEMPTER-3:

> If you want to live that badly, maybe you ought to go.

TEMPTER-2:

> Yes. We were wrong to discourage you. Go!

TEMPTER-3:

> Yes. Go!

TEMPTER-1:

> Please. Go!

TEMPTER-3:

> Just think: you may be giving up the solitude and quiet of this tomb, but you'll be a public hero!

TEMPTER-2:

> No one has ever been raised from the dead before!

TEMPTER-1:

> You'll be one of a kind.

TEMPTER-3:

> Why, everyone will want to see you.

TEMPTER-1:

> Touch you.

TEMPTER-3:

> Know you.

TEMPTER-2:

People will pay money just to see if you're really alive.

TEMPTER-1:

You won't have to worry about an income. You can sell your memoirs.

TEMPTER-2:

Or go on a lecture tour.

TEMPTER-3:

Think of the revenues and concessions.

TEMPTER-1:

You might even get your own show in Rome at the Coliseum.

TEMPTER-2:

People will make pilgrimages to your tomb.

TEMPTER-3:

And if they ever write a gospel, they'll probably put you in it! (*All three Tempters begin bombarding Lazarus with words that keep crescendoing. Lazarus becomes increasingly agitated and confused. Finally Lazarus raises his hands in a sharp gesture and silences them as he shouts:* STOP!)

LAZARUS:

STOP!

JESUS:

(*Tenderly*) Lazarus, come forth. (*The Spirit gestures to Lazarus and he begins walking out of the tomb toward Jesus. Lazarus comes to Jesus as Jesus comes to Lazarus. They embrace. Then Jesus indicates to Lazarus that they need to move on. Jesus and Lazarus are preceded first by the Spirit, then the disciples. The Tempters follow Lazarus and Jesus at a distance. They all make their way back into the audience or congregation. Silence follows.*)

Finis

PROPS

1. One cassette recording containing the first four or five minutes of Beethoven's Fifth Symphony. You may need to record these four or five minutes a couple of times depending on how long it takes your troupe to perform the mimed part of this drama.
2. Six large placards reading:
   (a) THE RAISING OF LAZARUS;
   (b) THE BAD NEWS;
   (c) LAZARUS DIES;
   (d) JESUS MEETS MARTHA;
   (e) JESUS MEETS MARY;
   (f) JESUS DOES HIS STUFF.
3. One long, colored scarf which is held by Lazarus and used in his death scene.
4. One huge clown hammer.
5. One box of tissues or one roll of toilet paper, whichever will more humorously convey the incessant crying of Mary.

PRODUCTION NOTES

This drama was first performed at the Pacific School of Religion chapel as part of a Jesuit School of Theology Sunday liturgy during Lent. We were following the Cycle A readings. We performed it with eight people. Obviously some characters played two roles.

I encourage you to adapt this drama, along with the rest of the dramas in this collection, to your own congregations or classes. Always keep in mind the physical and human resources that you have to work with. Oftentimes the players themselves will come up with imaginative insights and production suggestions that will enhance the overall experience of the biblical drama.

It is imperative that the Critic be a surprise. This person is planted in the audience or congregation from the very beginning. When we first did this in the PSR chapel, our Critic was sitting near the center aisle and next to an elderly lady. When he stood up and said: "You mean that's it? There's nothing more?" She tugged at his arm and said: "Sit down, dear. They did the best they could." It was unplanned and unrehearsed participation by a member of the congregation that was brilliant. While you can't plan for this to always happen, don't be surprised if it occasionally does occur.

Don't be intimidated or frightened by the humor of this biblical story or this biblical drama. Professor Douglas Adams, who teaches at the Graduate Theological Union in Berkeley, once asked me to work with him at a Pastors' workshop that focused on the miracle stories. We were exploring the humorous potential of Jesus' miracle stories with the class.

After we had performed this biblical drama to a very appreciative and experienced group of preachers and pastors, one member of the class spoke up and said: "That was all great fun but do you think a congregation who saw this on Sunday would get the point of the story?" My response was: "If you are asking me, pastor, is that the only sermon/homily you can give on this miracle story, my answer is *no*. This is the dramatized sermon/homily that I would give at this time. There are a thousand more stories that can be told that will shed some different light on the countless meanings of this beautiful biblical passage."

There is more than humor in this drama but the humor is an essential ingredient. If we could step back for a moment and see what we do regularly to distort a genuine understanding of the miracle stories in Jesus' life and ministry, the humor of this drama will seem small when compared to all of that. The humor in the drama really comes primarily from a recognition and affirmation by the congregation or audience of what we have done to strangle all the real life of these stories or the countless ways we have imprisoned what is meant to be experienced as "good news" in them. The humor of this and other dramas frees people up a little bit so they can hear and experience familiar stories freshly. And in bringing new eyes, new ears and new hearts to these stories, we may just experience some of the life-giving humor and hope that these biblical stories contain.

REFLECTION QUESTIONS AND EXERCISES

1. With what character in this story do you most identify? Describe this character in detail. Remember that this is an imaginative description, so we are not dealing with "right" and "wrong." Artists throughout the centuries have captured the characters of biblical stories in very imaginative and yet very different ways. What is there about this character that evokes your imaginative identification? With what character in this story do you least identify? Describe this character in detail. What is there about this character that makes him/her difficult to identify with?

2. Cultural anthropologists tell us that myths are truths that rise to articulation in community (Mircea Eliade). Christianity, too, has its truths that find expression in her stories. Joseph Campbell, when interviewed by Bill Moyers in the television series, "The Power of Myth," said that, "This is the final secret of the myth—to teach you how to penetrate the labyrinth of life in such a way that its spiritual values come through." What "truths" or "spiritual values" do you or your group believe find expression in this story of "The Raising of Lazarus"?

3. In a marvelous document entitled *Fulfilled in Your Hearing: The Homily in the Sunday Assembly* (National Conference of Catholic Bishops, 1982), you will find a suggested group reflection process for scriptural readings. Three of the reflection questions they suggest are quite appropriate for *The Raising of Lazarus* and every other biblical story that appears in this volume. First, what "good news" do you hear in this story? What shape or shapes does this "good news" take? What "promise" or "hope" finds expression in this story? Second, what is the "brokenness" or "challenge" or "sin" that finds expression in this story? To what kind(s) of conversion are we being called through this biblical story? Third, what difference (if any) would it make if the contemporary "good news" (i.e., the "good news" that you or your reflection group discover in this biblical story) was applied to our contemporary "brokenness" or "challenge" or "sin"?

4. Is there anyone you know and love who is ill right now? How does their illness affect you? Can you or your reflection group make any sense out of the idea that God can be glorified through illness or death? What does this say to you and your group about God? What does it say to you or your group about the real nature of suffering and death?

Toward the beginning of this story, after he is told that Lazarus is ill, Jesus says: "This sickness will not end in death, but it is for God's glory so that through it the Son of God may be glorified." The Coventry Cathedral was destroyed in a German bombing raid during the Second World War. The New Cathedral was built almost literally out of its ashes. In a slide presentation at the Cathedral about its destruction and subsequent reconstruction, a haunting phrase appears: "This cathedral was destroyed to the glory of God." Both Jesus and this slide presentation speak of brokenness and glory. What do you or your group think this means? How do these words challenge our contemporary understandings and interpretations of suffering, disaster and death?

5. In the latter part of this biblical story three strong symbols appear: (a) the tomb, (b) the stone, and (c) the bindings. What do each of these symbolize for you in your life? What are "the tombs" you/we dwell in? What are "the stones" that keep us prisoners of these tombs? Who are the people or what are the places and experiences that "bind" us? Who are the people and what are some of the experiences that call us out of "tombs"? Who rolls away the "stones" in our life? Who are some of the people and what are some of the experiences that "unbind" us and help us leave our caves of death in order to come out into the light of new life?

6. In the synoptic gospels (Matt 4:1–11; Mk 1:12–13; and Lk 4:1–13), after Jesus is baptized he is driven out into the desert by the Spirit for forty days. There he experiences his temptations. In the biblical drama, as Jesus is calling Lazarus from death to life, Lazarus is tempted in four different ways. What shape do you or your reflection group think that the four temptations of

Lazarus take? How might these same temptations be operative in our own life?

At the end of Luke's account of "the temptation in the wilderness," the narration says: "Having exhausted all these ways of tempting him, the devil left him, to return at the appointed time" (Lk 4:13). What do you or your group think is meant by "the appointed time"? In the biblical drama, the three Tempters follow Jesus and Lazarus at a distance. Do you think Lazarus has seen the last of them? Why or why not? What do you or your group think might be "the appointed time" in Lazarus' life when he might very well run into them again?

7. T. S. Eliot, in his play, *Murder in the Cathedral,* has his protagonist Thomas Becket say, after being tempted the fourth time: "The last deceit is the worst treason/ To do the right thing for the wrong reason." Why do you or your reflection group think Lazarus comes out of the tomb?

Reflect on St. Paul's "Hymn to God's Love" (Rom 8:31–39). What light does St. Paul shed on the biblical story and the biblical drama through these verses? Keep in mind that we are dealing with a mystery here. Mysteries can never fully be comprehended. Do you find it mysterious that Jesus brings Lazarus back to life? In the biblical story and the biblical drama which is stronger: "love" or "death"? What reasons can you or your group come up with to account for this?

When writing to the Corinthian community (1 Cor 13:13), St. Paul said: "In short, there are three things that last: faith, hope and love; and the greatest of these is love." Have you ever experienced love drawing "life from death" in your own life or the life of someone you know? How do faith, hope and love find human expression in the biblical story and in the biblical drama? How do faith, hope and love find expression in your life and the lives of those around you?

8. Pick up John's gospel again and continue reading through the eleventh verse of the twelfth chapter. In John 11:53 we see the religious leaders come to the decision that Jesus must die. In John 12:11 we see those same religious leaders make a similar

decision about Lazarus. How do you and your reflection group react to these decisions to put Jesus and Lazarus to death? What have Jesus and Lazarus done to deserve the sentence of death? In drama, attitudes find expression in the behaviors of characters. Using this dramatic principle, what attitudes do you or your reflection group think are being expressed in the behaviors of Jesus, Lazarus and the religious leaders?

2. Healing Blind Bartimaeus

(Mark 10:46–52)

And they came to Jericho; and as he was leaving Jericho with his disciples and a great multitude, Bartimaeus, a blind beggar, the son of Timaeus, was sitting by the roadside. And when he heard that it was Jesus of Nazareth, he began to cry out and say, "Jesus, Son of David, have mercy on me!" And many rebuked him, telling him to be silent; but he cried out all the more, "Son of David, have mercy on me!" And Jesus stopped and said, "Call him." And they called the blind man, saying to him, "Take heart; rise, he is calling you." And throwing off his mantle he sprang up and came to Jesus. And Jesus said to him, "What do you want me to do for you?" And the blind man said to him, "Master, let me receive my sight." And Jesus said to him, "Go your way; your faith has made you well." And immediately he received his sight and followed him on the way.

Bartimaeus

CAST

Bartimaeus	Jesus
Poor Person	Disciple-1
Hungry Person	Disciple-2
Captive Person	Narrator
Elderly Person	Placard Bearer
Self	

[**Note:** This dramatization has five parts. Each is titled. You can use hand-held placards to visually announce the divisions of the dramatization. Choose whatever music you think would best evoke the mood of this dramatization. "Laura's Love Song" (instrumental parts) from the movie soundtrack of *The Children of Sanchez* is what I have used with this. Keep in mind that the first, second and fifth parts of this dramatization are mimed. The music should accompany the mimed parts and will greatly enhance the mime as well as create and communicate the mood. The stage directions are for the church this dramatization was originally performed in.]

PART ONE: THE BLINDING

[*The Placard Bearer comes out and shows the congregation a large placard reading* THE BLINDING. *After the congregation has had a chance to see this, the Placard Bearer exits with placard. The music begins.*]

27

1. Bartimaeus comes up the center aisle surveying all the sights to be seen. He delights in the sky, the flowers, the trees, all the beauty that surrounds him.

2. As Bartimaeus moves from the ground level to the first platform, he becomes aware of the first of five symbolic figures. This first person represents "the poor." The Poor Person lifts a hand towards Bartimaeus in supplication. The Poor Person wants a donation, a handout, anything. And the Poor Person is desperate. Bartimaeus is revolted by the presence of the Poor Person and gestures this by putting one forearm across his eyes while with the other arm he gestures the sight of the Poor Person away.

3. Bartimaeus next encounters the second symbolic figure who represents "the hungry." The Hungry Person holds his stomach which is aching. The Hungry Person lifts a hand toward Bartimaeus in a gesture of seeking some relief or help. Bartimaeus is sickened by this sight and once again does his twofold gesture, this time to the Hungry Person.

4. Next Bartimaeus encounters a symbolic figure representing those who are captive or imprisoned in any way. The Captive Person's arms are crossed at the wrists in a gesture of being bound. The Captive Person extends her hands to Bartimaeus' right side and Bartimaeus turns away. The Captive Person then moves to his left side and makes supplication again. Bartimaeus expresses his revulsion through his twofold gesture.

5. The fourth symbolic figure that Bartimaeus meets is the one who represents "the elderly, the lonely and forgotten." When Bartimaeus sees the Elderly Person, he once again feels uncomfortable. The Elderly Person extends both arms toward Bartimaeus in a pleading gesture for help. Bartimaeus turns away from the Elderly Person with his twofold gesture.

6. The last symbolic figure that Bartimaeus meets represents "the Self." Self simply holds up a mirror to Bartimaeus' face.

Bartimaeus looks in the mirror briefly then recoils in fear and disgust. The Self tries one side which Bartimaeus turns away from quickly. Self tries the other side where Bartimaeus angrily makes his twofold gesture of rejection.

7. Bartimaeus comes frantically down from the first platform to the floor near the congregation and begins physicalizing his agony from all he does not want to see. He does not want to see any of these symbolic figures and lifts his hands plaintively to heaven beseeching God to take all of these sights away. Bartimaeus does not want to see any of it because it is so disturbing to him.

PART TWO: THE BINDING

[*The Placard Bearer comes on and shows the congregation a large placard reading* THE BINDING. *After the congregation have had a chance to look at it, the Placard Bearer leaves with the placard.*]

8. Slowly Bartimaeus' face becomes relieved and somewhat peaceful. Slowly it becomes clear to the congregation that Bartimaeus has been blinded. He has prayed not to see any of this pain and misery and his prayer has been answered. But Bartimaeus is now blind.

9. Now Bartimaeus will begin to experience the same rejection that he has meted out. First, Bartimaeus experiences poverty and imitates the posture and gestures of the Poor Person. The two people who later become The Disciples in the dramatization work now as the Passers-by who reject Bartimaeus in his need. Bartimaeus lifts his hand to beg some small help but is rejected by Disciple-1. Disciple-1 uses the same gesture of rejection that Bartimaeus had used earlier.

10. Next Bartimaeus becomes hungry and imitates the posture and gestures of the Hungry Person. Bartimaeus holds out both hands in supplication to Disciple-2 but is rejected.

11. Bartimaeus then angrily slams his fists together and his wrists become bound. He begins to panic and becomes frightened. Bartimaeus lifts his bound hands in supplication to Disciple-1 who spurns him.

12. Dejected, Bartimaeus brings his hands down to his face and begins to weep. His shoulders begin to stoop. A limp gradually appears in his walk. Bartimaeus lifts his open arms in a plea for help to Disciple-2 who rejects him.

13. Finally, Bartimaeus takes out a little mirror from his clothing and holds it up to Disciple-1 who spurns him. Bartimaeus does the same thing to Disciple-2 who also rejects him. The Disciples depart (right) and leave Bartimaeus dejected and alone.

PART THREE: THE QUESTION

[*This part of the dramatization begins with the choir and congregation singing "Son of David, Have Pity On Me" by John Foley, S.J.. Another appropriate song can be substituted. This song comes from the St. Louis Jesuits' album entitled* Wood Hath Hope. *Each time the antiphon is sung it builds in volume and intensity. Bartimaeus is huddled on the floor during this. The Placard Bearer comes on and shows the congregation a large placard which reads* THE QUESTION. *After the congregation has had a chance to see this, the Placard Bearer leaves with the placard. The choir and congregation then begin their singing of "Son of David, Have Pity On Me."*]

NARRATOR:

They came to Jericho next, and as Jesus was leaving that place with his disciples and a sizable crowd, there was a blind beggar Bartimaeus, son of Timaeus, sitting by the roadside.

BARTIMAEUS:

What's all the commotion? (*He tugs at someone's leg.*) What's all the excitement about?

DISCIPLE-2:

Jesus of Nazareth is leaving town.

BARTIMAEUS:

Oh yeah? Well, what's so special about him?

DISCIPLE-2:

The spirit of God is upon him. He feeds the hungry with his wisdom and compassion. He speaks a word of hope to the poor. He heals those who are broken in body and heart. He has announced that the reign of God is near.

DISCIPLE-1:

Hush! Here comes Jesus now!

BARTIMAEUS:

(*As Jesus begins walking past Bartimaeus and down the aisle, Bartimaeus speaks up.*) Jesus, Son of David, have pity on me!

DISCIPLE-1:

Hey, old man, knock it off! What do you want to do, ruin his visit here?

DISCIPLE-2:

Yes, would you please shut up?

BARTIMAEUS:

(*He is even more insistent now.*) Jesus, Son of David, have pity on me!

DISCIPLES-1&2:
Shuuusssssshhhhhhh!!!!!

JESUS:

(*Jesus stops midway down the aisle.*) Call that person over here.

DISCIPLE-1:

You have nothing to fear from this Jesus!

DISCIPLE-2:

Get up! He is calling you. (*Bartimaeus jumps up. Disciple-1 and Disciple-2 help Bartimaeus come to Jesus.*)

JESUS:

What do you want me to do for you? (*Everyone but Bartimaeus freezes. Bartimaeus comes toward the congregation.*)

PART FOUR: THE ANSWER

[*The Placard Bearer comes on and shows the congregation a large placard that reads* THE ANSWER. *After the congregation has seen this, the Placard Bearer leaves with the placard.*]

BARTIMAEUS:

What do I want? What on earth do I want? (*Bartimaeus thinks for a moment and then his face begins to light up.*) I think I want to see.

POOR:

So you think you want to see, do you? Once before you could see, and much of what you saw disgusted you. You prayed then that you wouldn't have to see all those things in this world that disturbed and unsettled you. Your prayer was answered. You now know our darkness and our pain.

BARTIMAEUS:

But who are you?

POOR:

We are the voices of the poor and the helpless.

HUNGRY:

We are the voices of those who hunger and thirst for nourishment and satisfaction.

CAPTIVE:

We are the desperate voices of all those unjustly bound and oppressed.

ELDERLY:

We are the anguished cries of the lost and forgotten, all those pushed aside and put away because we remind you of the fragility of life.

SELF:

We are the voices that clamor within you. We are your deepest fears revealed. We are the ashes of your shattered dreams.

ALL:

Do you really want to see, Bartimaeus?

BARTIMAEUS:

I don't know. I'm confused. I think I want to see. I really do!

POOR:

And with your sight, how much of me will you take in? Will you stand with me in my helplessness? Can you make room in your mind for different ways of thinking? Can you make room in your heart for strange and frightening feelings? Can you make room in your life for the stranger who is poor in so many ways?

BARTIMAEUS:

Yes, I do want to see you! (*The Poor Person makes a healing gesture over Bartimaeus' face and goes to a position in front of Jesus.*)

HUNGRY:

Once before you turned away from me, Bartimaeus. Will you listen to the pleas of the starving all around you? Do you have the courage to experience and share my hunger and thirst for acceptance, for companionship, for healing, for love?

BARTIMAEUS:

Yes, I want to see you too! (*The Hungry Person makes a healing gesture over Bartimaeus' face and goes to a position in front of the Poor Person.*)

CAPTIVE:

Will you turn away from me, Bartimaeus? Will you forget me when your sight returns?

BARTIMAEUS:

Who are you?

CAPTIVE:

I am all you do not know and therefore fear. I am the voice of all those bound because of fear and ignorance. You say you want to see me, but do you really want to see and share my pain, the pain of being caricatured and disregarded because of my sex, my color, my feelings, my situation in life?

BARTIMAEUS:

Yes, I do want to see not part but all of life. (*The Captive Person makes a healing gesture over Bartimaeus' face and goes to a position in front of the Hungry Person.*)

ELDERLY:

Do you want to see all of us who are not born or have not died struggle desperately for love and life? Do you want to see all those for whom you have a word of judgment but no word of grace? Do you want to see all those for whom you have no thought, no feeling, no word at all?

BARTIMAEUS:

Yes, I do want to see all of this, all of you! (*The Elderly Person makes a healing gesture over Bartimaeus' face and goes to a position in front of the Captive Person.*)

SELF:

Are you willing to look inside of yourself as well? Are you willing to see how ugliness and beauty, darkness and light live in the same house within you? Are you willing to focus not on what you don't have but on the genuine gifts that have been given to you? Do you want vision that will constantly call you to a "change of heart" toward yourself and others?

BARTIMAEUS:

With all my heart I do! (*Self makes a healing gesture over Bartimaeus' face and goes to a position in front of the Elderly Person. Bartimaeus then goes back into the scene with Jesus as Jesus and the Disciples come alive again.*)

JESUS:

What do you want me to do for you?

BARTIMAEUS:

Teacher, I want to see again.

JESUS:

Be on your way. Your faith has healed you. (*At this point, each of the symbolic figures has been standing with their hands in front of and covering their faces. After Jesus says this, each one goes down on his/her knees into a squatting position and uncovers his/her face. Bartimaeus reaches out for Jesus. In turn, each of the symbolic figures stand aside as they pull Bartimaeus closer and closer to Jesus. When Bartimaeus reaches Jesus, Jesus embraces him.*)

PART FIVE: THE ROAD

[*The Placard Bearer comes on and shows the congregation a large placard that reads* THE ROAD. *After the congregation have seen this, the Placard Bearer leaves with the placard.*]

14. After Jesus has embraced Bartimaeus, Jesus begins to exit down the center aisle. Halfway down, Jesus turns to Bartimaeus who has been watching intently. Bartimaeus starts to follow Jesus.

15. When Bartimaeus starts to follow Jesus, he gets as far as the first few pews and then stops. He turns and looks back at the symbolic figures. Then Bartimaeus looks at Jesus. Bartimaeus then goes back and gets the symbolic figures. Bartimaeus stands in the middle of them.

16. Once Bartimaeus has gotten them, together they follow Jesus down the aisle and out.

Finis

PROPS

1. Five large placards reading:
   (a) THE BLINDING;
   (b) THE BINDING;
   (c) THE QUESTION;
   (d) THE ANSWER;
   (e) THE ROAD.
2. One cassette recording of the instrumental portions of "Laura's Love Song" from the movie soundtrack of *The Children of Sanchez*.
3. One handle mirror for the character Self.

PRODUCTION NOTES

This dramatization of Jesus' healing of "The Blind Man of Jericho" (Mark 10:46–52) was first performed as a dramatized sermon on the thirtieth Sunday of the year in Cycle B. The theme of this biblical story and biblical drama also make it uniquely appropriate for use during the seasons of Advent and Lent. In its present format it could easily be incorporated as part of a communal celebration of reconciliation during these "seasons of preparation."

Each of the dramas in this collection was the result of a faith-sharing process. While I ultimately gave the drama written form, each member of the Biblical Explorers, through their weekly reflection, presence and creative improvisational work genuinely influenced the shape of each of these dramatizations.

When you are working with your liturgy group or reflection group, I encourage you to let them make these biblical dramas their own through the dramatic production suggestions and choices they make. For instance, your group may come up with far better ways to dramatically communicate the five symbolic characters of this drama to a congregation or audience than we did. While simplicity should always be a goal in doing these dramas, the simplicity of our productions was oftentimes dictated by the little time we had to rehearse them. Remember that every time your group makes a decision (the way a character should be captured or an action/attitude conveyed), they also make an investment. Through these investments the drama genuinely becomes the product of their faith and imagination and not just ours.

If you use this dramatization as the homily/sermon of a liturgy, I think it is important to follow it with some moments of silent reflection. It could be quite effective during the Prayers of the Faithful to have the five symbolic characters voice a prayer that embodies the concerns and condition of the people their character represents (i.e., the poor, the hungry, the captive, the elderly, or some aspect of the self) in your community. If you do this, you might consider having Bartimaeus voice a concluding prayer as well.

REFLECTION QUESTIONS AND EXERCISES

1. The story about *The Healing of Blind Bartimaeus* (Mk 10: 46–52) comes from a section of Mark's gospel (Mk 8:22–10:52) that contemporary scripture scholars believe focuses on Jesus' instructing his followers about his identity (Christology) and what it means to follow him (discipleship). (See *The New Jerome*

Biblical Commentary, New Jersey: Prentice Hall, Inc., 1990, especially Daniel J. Harrington's contribution on "The Gospel According To Mark.")

This part of Mark's gospel begins and ends with the healing of a blind man (Mk 8:22–26 and Mk 10:46–52). In this section of Mark's gospel, Jesus makes three predictions about his passion and immediately follows these with instructions to his followers about what it means to be a disciple.

I encourage you or your study group to reflect on each of these predictions of the passion and subsequent teachings by Jesus on what it means to be his follower. What do you or your group think it means to be a disciple of Jesus from the first prediction of the passion and its consequences for discipleship? (Mk 8:31–38) What do you or your reflection group think it means to be a disciple of Jesus in light of the second prediction of the passion and its consequences for discipleship? (Mk 9:30–50) What do you or your reflection group think it means to be a disciple of Jesus from the third prediction of the passion and its consequences for discipleship? (Mk 10:32–45) How do you follow Christ in a consumer society? (John Kavanaugh's book *Following Christ in a Consumer Society* can be an excellent resource for you and your reflection group. It is also available from Paulist Press. Orbis Press has an excellent book by Albert Nolan entitled *Jesus Before Christianity.* Both books will provide disturbing and challenging reflection material for you and your group on what it means to be a follower (disciple) of Jesus in contemporary culture and society.)

2. In this section of Mark's gospel (Mk 8:22–10:52), Jesus is telling the disciples that to follow him means to enter with him in his suffering, dying and rising. St. Ignatius of Loyola in his *Spiritual Exercises* has a meditation on "Christ the King and His Call" at the beginning of the second week. [*The Spiritual Exercises,* translated by Elder Mullan, S.J., in David L. Fleming, S.J., *The Spiritual Exercises of St. Ignatius: A Literal Translation and A Contemporary Reading* (St. Louis: Institute of Jesuit Sources, 1978).]

Prayerfully reflect on this meditation of St. Ignatius. What do Christ's words, "It is my will to conquer the whole world and all my enemies, and thus to enter into the glory of my Father. Therefore, whoever wishes to join me in this enterprise must be willing to labor with me, that by following me in suffering, he may follow me in glory," mean to you or your reflection group?

A few years ago, in a Campus Ministry teleconference that explored how to celebrate Holy Week, one panelist suggested that on Good Friday communities should physically visit and pray in those places in their city where Christ is suffering and dying. He went on to suggest that, in order to incorporate the entire paschal mystery into such Holy Week celebrations, the same communities should physically visit and give thanks on Easter Sunday for those places in their city where Christ is coming to new life. Where do you or your reflection group think Christ is suffering and dying in your school, in your church, in your city, in the world today? Where do you or your reflection group think that Christ is coming to new life in your school, in your church, in your city, in the world today?

3. A cinquain is a five-line piece of poetry. The first line consists of the word that is the title or subject of your poetic reflection. The second line consists of two descriptive adjectives that deal with your subject. The third line consists of three present participles (action words, verbs ending in "ing") that capture active dimensions of your first line subject. The fourth line consists in a four word descriptive summary of your subject. The fifth line consists in a one-word restatement of your first line subject. The final word (line) usually brings out some nuanced dimension of the original first word and is an emphatic or gentle restatement of it.

After you and your reflection group have explored the possibilities of the first question, I would like each of you to compose a cinquain on the theme of discipleship. The first word of each of your cinquains will be "discipleship." Each of you must come up with the other four lines. When you have all had a chance to compose these, share them with the entire group. After doing this, I encourage you to try and compose a group cinquain on "discipleship" that incorporates a number of the insights of your group.

4. What does Bartimaeus' blindness symbolize for you or your reflection group? What are some of the ways in which we, in our culture and society are blind today? I suggest you consider this reflection question in terms of awareness and response. How aware and concerned are we about the struggles of our brothers and sisters in other parts of the world? What are the struggles of our brothers and sisters in Northern Ireland? What are some of the struggles of our brothers and sisters in eastern Europe? What do our brothers and sisters in Ethiopia or the Sudan struggle with? What are some of the struggles that our brothers and sisters in El Salvador or Central America wrestle with every day? What are some of the struggles we are not aware of? How can our blindness add to their pain? Given your awareness of your brothers and sisters in different parts of the world, how can you or your reflection group practically and concretely respond to these struggles? This calls for courageous and creative brainstorming on your part.

5. There is an Hasidic story about "compassion" that goes something like this. A rabbi told his congregation that he discovered the real meaning of love by overhearing the conversation of two villagers. The first villager said: "My friend, do you love me?" To which the second villager responded: "Of course I love you." The first villager said: "Do you know, my friend, what brings me pain?" The second, somewhat confused, responded: "How can I know what brings you pain?" The first villager then concluded: "If you do not know what brings me pain, how can you say that you really love me?" The rabbi then told his congregation: "Know then, my people, that to love, to really love, means to know what brings your comrade pain." (Quoted in *Hasidic Anthology* by Louis I. Newman, New York: Schocken Books, 1963, p. 221.)

In light of this, I encourage you or your reflection group to consider the following questions. What brings women in our church and our workplace pain? What brings people who are "differently abled" pain in our schools and our society today? What brings the elderly pain in our culture and society today? How does ignorance or apathy hold different groups of people in our society captive today? Awareness and insight precede compassionate actions and response. If you or your reflection group know what brings pain to any of these groups of your brothers and sisters, brainstorm on some of the ways we might compassionately respond to their pain. What can you do as an individual? What can you do as a group? Remember what Lao-tsu said: "A journey of three thousand miles is begun with one step." What is one step you or your reflection group could take to ease the pain of one of these groups of your brothers and sisters?

6. There are five symbolic figures in this biblical dramatization. Initially, Bartimaeus did not want to see them. What are we blinded to in our society and culture today? Who are the people we don't want to see? What are the things, the events, the realities that we would prefer to turn a "blind eye" to rather than be disturbed by the sight of them? What do the five symbolic figures represent for you or your reflection group in our culture and society today?

To assist you in these reflections, I encourage you or your reflection group to imaginatively consider how television commercials and newsprint advertising present these five symbolic figures in our culture and society? Do you ever see the "poor" or "hungry" or "elderly" in advertising? How are they represented, if represented at all? Can the "poor" or "homeless" buy the products that commercial advertising markets? Is advertising, then, interested in them? Do you find the ways the elderly are portrayed in television and magazine advertising appealing? Do you look forward to your skin wrinkling and your hair turning grey? How do you feel about the possibility of losing your teeth or developing problems with "regularity"? Can you or your reflection group think of any positive aspects to growing old? It would be of tremendous assistance to have some older members in your reflection group share their experiences of growing older or have members of your reflection group talk to their older relatives and friends and share what they discover with the whole group. They would have a wealth of experience to draw upon and share with the group on all the issues your group considers. Is there possibly more to the "aging process" than contemporary advertising represents? Why or why not? Explain.

What do the symbolic figures of the "captive" and the "self" represent to you or your reflection group? What images of the "captive" or the "self" does contemporary advertising give us in our culture and society today. Are these accurate or inaccurate? Why? Explain.

7. This is a journal exercise. You will need a quiet place, a Bible, a writing instrument and some paper or a journal in which to record your reflections. Quiet yourself down. You can often-times do this by paying attention to your breathing. Take in some large breaths of air and slowly let them out. Gradually slow your breathing down. When you feel calm, slowly read over the mira-cle story in Mark's gospel, "The Healing of Blind Bartimaeus" (Mk 10:46–52). Imagine that Jesus is in the room with you. Hear him say to you what scripture reports that he said to Bartimaeus: "What do you want me to do for you?" (Mk 10:51) Write down the first thing that comes into your mind in response to this ques-tion. Hear Jesus repeat the question to you. Each time he asks that question, write down the next thing that comes to mind. Continue this until you feel you have exhausted your responses. Now look at everything you have written down and reflect on all that you would ask Jesus to do for you.

8. In the biblical dramatization, what is the first thing Bar-timaeus sees after his sight returns? Why do you or your reflec-tion group think that the five symbolic figures stand between Jesus and Bartimaeus? What do you or your reflection group think is the significance, after he is healed by Jesus, of having Bartimaeus go back to the symbolic figures and bring them with him as he follows Jesus "on the way"? How will the presence of these five symbolic figures help Bartimaeus experience and view life differently?

3. Exorcising a Demon

(Mark 5:1-20)

They came to the other side of the sea, to the country of the Gerasenes. And when he had come out of the boat, there met him out of the tombs a man with an unclean spirit, who lived among the tombs; and no one could bind him any more, even with a chain; for he had often been bound with fetters and chains, but the chains he wrenched apart, and the fetters he broke in pieces; and no one had the strength to subdue him. Night and day among the tombs and on the mountains he was always crying out, and bruising himself with stones. And when he saw Jesus from afar, he ran and worshiped him;

and crying out with a loud voice, he said, "What have you to do with me, Jesus, Son of the Most High God? I adjure you by God, do not torment me." For he had said to him, "Come out of the man, you unclean spirit!" And Jesus asked him, "What is your name?" He replied, "My name is Legion; for we are many." And he begged him eagerly not to send them out of the country. Now a great herd of swine was feeding there on the hillside; and they begged him, "Send us to the swine, let us enter them." So he gave them leave. And the unclean spirits came out, and entered the swine; and the herd, numbering about two thousand, rushed down the steep bank into the sea, and were drowned in the sea.

The herdsmen fled, and told it in the city and in the country. And people came to see what it was that had happened. And they came to Jesus, and saw the demoniac sitting there, clothed and in his right mind, the man who had had the legion; and they were afraid. And those who had seen it told what had happened to the demoniac and to the swine. And they began to beg Jesus to depart from their neighborhood. And as he was getting into the boat, the man who had been possessed with demons begged him that he might be with him. But he refused, and said to him, "Go home to your friends, and tell them how much the Lord has done for you, and how he has had mercy on you." And he went away and began to proclaim in the Decapolis how much Jesus had done for him; and everyone marveled.

It's a Long Rope to Freedom

CAST

Gloria (An outcast)
Karl (An outcast)
Dizzy (An outcast)
Grandpa (An outcast)
Child (An outcast)
Yvette (An outcast)
Charles O'Currant (An outcast)
Betsy the Bag Lady (An outcast)
Lyndon LaGoof (An incast)

Martha (An incast)
George (An incast)
Priscilla (An incast)
Miles (An incast)
Donde (An outcast)
Narrator

NARRATOR:

Once upon a time, during the darker ages, a time of prejudice and persecution, a tiny band of our eight-parents. . . .

AUDIENCE:

Eight-parents?

NARRATOR:

Yes, eight-parents. That's foremothers and forefathers! A
tiny band of our eight-parents left a land of oppression, the
only home they had known, and set out to find a new home
of freedom and justice. After forty weeks of days and nights
at sea, the little band of pilgrims finally landed on a deserted
island that was to become their new home.

LYNDON:

Friends, this is our new home.

45

DIZZY:
We have left a land of death.

GLORIA:
May we build here, in this place, a land of life . . .

GRANDPA:
. . . of community . . .

YVETTE:
. . . of dignity.

MILES:
We have left a land of oppression.

MARTHA:
May we build here a land of freedom . . .

GEORGE:
. . . of opportunity . . .

PRISCILLA:
. . . of equality.

CHARLES:
We have left a land of intolerance and sorrow.

GRANDPA:
May we build here a land of compassion . . .

YVETTE:
. . . of healing . . .

MILES:
. . . of service . . .

CHILD:
. . . and happiness!

LYNDON:

Let these ropes that bound us for so long now be a constant reminder of our commitment to work together to make of this land a place of life, freedom and happiness for ourselves and all who come after us.

NARRATOR:

They decided to name their dream and call the place: "Graceland." Things went along swimmingly well for the first few months. And then, one day, a boat arrived carrying three people who were tired, poor, and huddled together seeking safety and a new home.

CHILD:

Welcome, strangers.

GRANDPA:

Yes, welcome to Graceland.

PRISCILLA:

Not so fast, grandpa! I think we should find out a few things before we open our arms wide to this wretched refuse from some teeming shore!

MILES:

Priscilla has a point. Does anyone know who these people are? Has anyone checked their papers?

MARTHA:

Just what are your names?

GEORGE:

And why have you come here?

KARL:

My name is Karl and I heard this was a land where you shared all things in common.

MILES:
But why did you leave *your* "place of origin?"

KARL:
I didn't exactly leave. I was thrown out.

PRISCILLA:
Why?

KARL:
Because I believed that the rights of the few were not as important as the needs of the many.

LYNDON:
(*To incasts*) This could mean BIG trouble. He sounds like a communist agitator to me.

BETSY:
My name is Betsy. I came here because I have no home to call my own, no place to lay my head.

MARTHA:
And what do you do for a living, Betsy?

BETSY:
I collect things people throw away.

PRISCILLA:
You might have a hard time making a living here, Betsy, since we believe strongly in the principle: "Waste not, want not!" You see, my dear, *here* we don't throw things away.

DONDE:
My name is Donde. I am a hunter.

GEORGE:
And what do you hunt, Mr. Donde?

DONDE:

I hunt crocodiles.

MILES:

May we see your papers?

DONDE:

Papers? I don't need no stinking papers!

LYNDON:

No papers, no shirt, no shoes, NO HOME!

KARL:

Just who are you?

CHARLES:

That's our Minister of Quality Control: Lyndon LaGoof!

BETSY:

We came here because we heard this was a land of opportunity, a place where people could find acceptance, tolerance and hospitality.

DONDE:

We weren't expecting this type of treatment.

LYNDON:

Well, Mr. Donde, we have to draw the line somewhere. If we accepted everyone who came to these shores we would be overrun with undesirables in no time at all! I'm afraid you and Betsy and Karl will simply have to go! We have no place for you here.

DONDE:

If not you, who? If not here, where? If not now, when?

LYNDON:

I don't know! I don't care! And frankly, my dear, it's not our concern. (*Betsy begins to cry.*)

CHILD:
(*Crosses to Betsy.*) Now look what you've done to her.

GRANDPA:
(*Crosses to Betsy.*) Have we all forgotten so quickly?

DIZZY:
(*Crosses to Donde.*) Which of us had papers when we came to Graceland?

YVETTE:
(*Crosses to Donde.*) Is it lack of papers or the color of his skin that makes Donde unacceptable here?

GLORIA:
(Crosses to Karl.) Do we all have to agree with LaGoof?

CHARLES:
(*Crosses to Karl.*) Aren't we strong enough to entertain disagreement among ourselves?

GRANDPA:
Wasn't Graceland to be a place of freedom for all?

YVETTE:
If our vision of freedom doesn't grow, it will surely die.

MARTHA:
You're right.

GEORGE:
You should be free.

PRISCILLA:
We should be free.

MILES:
You should be free to leave . . .

LYNDON:

... and we should be free to throw you out!

NARRATOR:

(As the outcasts are making their way to another part of the stage, Betsy the bag lady begins picking up the pieces of rope that the incasts take off their wrists and throw away.)

And so the Outcasts of Graceland left. They slowly made their way out of the Incast's sight. They traveled to a remote part of the island where they once again began to build a new home. The first weeks and months were difficult. But they gradually learned how to rely on one another. The tragedy that initially evoked anger and resentment in them became the occasion for discovering and calling forth hidden gifts and new ways to serve one another. Through their living and working and playing together they uncovered those gifts that would build and sustain a community of freedom. Gloria shared the gift of hospitality. She could make everyone feel welcome. Charles O'Currant had the gift of curiosity. He taught the others how to treasure their questions. Grandpa showed the others how to remember the wisdom and truth only found in stories. Dizzy's vulnerability unlocked compassion in the hearts of all. Karl's respect for the needs of the many challenged them to new depths of sharing. Betsy continued to seek and find value in what others discarded. Crocodile Donde offered courage and great hope in the face of many obstacles. The child's enthusiasm, vision and zest for life often revived their drooping spirits. And Yvette sang. *(The group closes together, joins in song, with big smile revealing their joy.)*

The community of New Graceland was growing and thriving until one day the child noticed something.

CHILD:

Look, the waters are rising.

CHARLES:

Is that good news or bad news?

GRANDPA:
That depends on how well you can swim, young fellah!

DIZZY:
I can't swim.

BETSY:
Neither can I.

YVETTE:
What are we going to do?

DONDE:
I know we'll think of something. It's on the tip of my tongue.

GLORIA:
Open your mouth, Donde, and stick out your tongue.
That's it!

DONDE:
What did you find?

GLORIA:
We have to get to higher ground. We'll be safe there!

DONDE:
That was in my mouth. I knew it was there!

CHARLES:
Potential problem, folks. Those are pretty steep cliffs. How
will we be able to get up them?

KARL:
Few, if any, of us could get there on our own. Together, however, I think we can all make it to safety.

YVETTE:
How?

KARL:

> Look at what Betsy is doing with those discarded pieces of rope. She's forming a chain with her pieces of rope. Why can't we make a human chain?

DONDE:

> Yeah, why not? Let's give it a try.

NARRATOR:

> To the surprise and relief of all, the wisdom and resources of Donde, Betsy and Karl helped the inhabitants of New Graceland to safety and dry ground.

CHILD:

> Whew! We made it! I don't think I'll ever forget that close call.

GRANDPA:

> I hope none of us ever forgets this day.

GLORIA:

> Let these ropes be a constant reminder of our commitment to work together hand in hand to make of this land a place of life, freedom, and happiness for ourselves and all who come after us.

NARRATOR:

> While the Outcasts began carving out a new life for themselves on higher, dryer ground, the Incasts grew desperate as the water continued to rise.

GEORGE:

> Well, Martha, this is another fine mess you've gotten me into!

MARTHA:

> Don't start nagging, George. You know how I hate your nagging.

MILES:

Yeah. She's not in charge of "Quality Control" around here.

PRISCILLA:

(*To Lyndon*) O.K. Mr. Know-It-All, what are you going to do to get us out of this?

LYNDON:

Shush! I'm thinking!

PRISCILLA:

What are you thinking?

LYNDON:

I'm thinking we are in BIG TROUBLE. Anyone got any bright ideas? There's dry ground up above, but it's so steep I don't see how we can ever get there.

MARTHA:

Wait a minute. What happened to all of those people we threw out of Graceland?

GEORGE:

They probably drowned . . .

LYNDON:

. . . OR they found a way to higher, dryer ground. That's it! Let's look for them.

NARRATOR:

And so the tiny band of Incasts scoured the island searching for the Outcasts. Exhausted and just about ready to give up, they heard the sounds of music coming from above them. They looked up and saw the Outcasts. They began screaming for all they were worth!

INCASTS:

Help! Help! Save us or we'll drown!

YVETTE:
Do you see what I see?

GLORIA:
If we don't help them, they are going to drown!

KARL:
The water has risen too much. Our human chain would be too dangerous.

CHILD:
But we have to do something. We have to help them up here to safety.

CHARLES:
And what if, once they're safe, they throw us out again? We may be asking for more trouble than we can deal with in helping them.

DIZZY:
Let's cross that bridge when we come to it. What they need now is not our reservations but our help.

DONDE:
If we excluded them we would be no different than them.

YVETTE:
But how are we going to get them from there to here?

GLORIA:
There must be some way. We must have some resource we've forgotten.

GRANDPA:
That's it.

OUTCASTS:
What's it?

GRANDPA:

We've forgotten.

OUTCASTS:

Forgotten what?

GRANDPA:

Our pieces of rope that remind us of our hopes and dreams for New Graceland.

CHILD:

But Grandpa, the ropes aren't strong enough to lift them to safety.

BETSY:

Individually, they aren't strong enough, child. But if we weave them together they can create a lifeline for any endangered neighbors.

GRANDPA:

Remember our hopes? Remember our dreams? Remember the kind of home we committed ourselves to build? Remember our promise never, never to allow what happened to us to happen again to anyone who came to New Graceland?

KARL:

Will we be people of the truth or people of the lie?

NARRATOR:

The Incasts waited helplessly and hopefully on the beach below. One by one, the Outcasts took off their ropes of remembrance. Betsy began weaving them into a lifeline that could bring up their neighbors to the safety and shelter of dry ground. As the Outcasts slowly lowered the lifeline to their neighbors below, they saw the outline of countless tiny boats dotting the horizon. They were all headed in the direction of New Graceland.

Finis

PROPS

1. Thirty pieces of colored yarn. A colored piece of yarn is worn around each character's wrist. It is long enough to suggest "chains" that have been broken.
2. Multiple pieces of colored yarn. Each member of the congregation or audience is given a piece of yarn when they enter. These will hopefully arouse curiosity about their significance before the biblical drama and afterwards serve as reminders ("memory joggers") of what they have seen.
3. Hats or props to help capture different characters. Betsy the Bag Lady could have a shopping cart. Minimally she would need a large plastic garbage bag to gather into it all the things that others discard. Grandpa might use a cane and wear a large, baggy sweater.

PRODUCTION NOTES

This biblical drama was originally done as a dramatized homily in a worship service at Santa Clara University's Mission Church. It was part of a liturgy series sponsored by Campus Ministry entitled: "Christianity: A Road To Freedom."

We gave each member of the congregation a ten-inch piece of colored yarn as they came in the Mission Church. This aroused curiosity in many of them. The significance and meaning of the pieces of yarn was underscored by the presence of colored yarn on the wrists of each of the characters in the biblical dramatization. For weeks after this liturgy and series on "Christian Freedom," members of the congregation could be seen around campus wearing their colored pieces of yarn on their wrists. While it is open to interpretation just exactly why so many could be seen wearing the colored yarn, I believe at least some of them wanted to remember and deepen in themselves awareness of the freedom that had been given symbolic expression in those colored pieces of yarn.

This biblical dramatization does not call for numerous props or costumes. I encourage you to have your drama group use their imaginations and brainstorm how they might best visually communicate the different characters in this dramatization. As always, the prop or costume can only assist each person in their embodiment and communication of a character. It will take personal reflection and investment on each person's part to capture the essence of their character. Be guided in this by an adapted Ignatian principle. To the extent a costume or prop helps you authentically capture and communicate your character, use it. To the extent that a costume or prop distracts you from genuinely capturing and communicating your character, don't use it.

REFLECTION QUESTIONS AND EXERCISES

1. In the theater and in life characters reveal who they are by what they say and what they do. I invite you or your reflection group to consider the following questions: Who does Jesus reveal himself to be through his words and actions in this miracle story? Who does the Gerasene Demoniac reveal himself to be through his words and actions in this story? Who do the townspeople reveal themselves to be through their words and actions in this story? In the passage immediately preceding this one, in Mark's gospel, Jesus was in a boat with his disciples weathering a storm. Where are the disciples throughout the dialogue and action of this story? Who do the disciples reveal themselves to be through what they say and what they do in this story? Now let us shift the focus a bit. If people observed what you said and what you did, who would they say you revealed yourself to be through these words and actions?

2. What hope, what healing or "good news" do you or your reflection group hear in this miracle story? What brokenness, what fracturing or "sin" do you or your reflection group hear in this story? To what kind(s) of conversion are we being called? In light of this gospel story, "what" are we to change or "how" are we to change in order to follow the example and teaching of Christ more faithfully? What difference, if any, would it make if this contemporary "good news" was applied to contemporary "bad news"?

3. In a dream, every element or character represents some part or aspect of yourself. Even when your dreams are peopled by family, friends, cinematic characters or strangers, every one of them represents/symbolizes some part of you. And you are ultimately the only one who can interpret your dream. I would like to invite you or your reflection group to do an imaginative journal exercise. I want you to approach this miracle story with this understanding and brief background about dreams. Go through this miracle story and write down every character or element that appears in the story. What if every character or element in this story represented some aspect or part of you. What does each character or element of the biblical story represent/symbolize in you or your reflection group? (i.e., what possesses or preoccupies you? Who is the Christ in you?) Take your time and consider each character and element of this story.

4. The *Spiritual Exercises* of St. Ignatius of Loyola have been described as "a method of helping Christians discover how God is calling them to live in deeper faith and greater freedom." (*Life In Faith And Freedom* by Edouard Pousset, S.J., St. Louis: Institute of Jesuit Sources, 1980. From the "Translator's Preface," p. xiii.) "The First Principle and Foundation" (No. 23) and "The Three Classes of Men" (No. 149) are examples of a consideration and a meditation that explore the nature of freedom for the person in relationship with God. I invite you or your reflection group to consider these "spiritual exercises" one at a time. How do you or your reflection group think these "spiritual exercises" might help Christians discover how God is "calling them to live in deeper faith and greater freedom"?

5. France gave the United States a symbol of freedom. It is the Statue of Liberty. These words of Emma Lazarus are found on the statue: "Give me your tired, your poor, your huddled masses yearning to breathe free, the wretched refuse of your teeming shore. Send these the homeless, tempest tossed to me. I lift my lamp beside the golden door." How did you or your reflection group's immigrant ancestors experience the truth of these words? Attitudes find expression in behaviors. What do you or your reflection group think are current American attitudes and

behaviors toward prospective groups who wish to immigrate to the United States? Are these attitudes and behaviors the same toward all prospective ethnic groups? Why or why not? Explain. How adequately do you or your reflection group think that these words on the Statue of Liberty capture the attitudes and behaviors of Americans today?

6. In the biblical drama, what do the pieces of colored yarn represent? What do the Incasts do with these pieces of yarn? Why do they do this? What do the Outcasts do with these pieces of yarn? Why do they do this? What are some symbolic objects that you or members of your reflection group have that remind them of their history (i.e., who they are, the struggles endured, where they came from, what they have inherited ethnically or religiously from ancestors who have gone before them, etc.)?

What kind of place do the first inhabitants of Graceland hope to build? What qualities do they hope will characterize their new home? What do you or your reflection group think of these qualities? Why do the Incasts throw the Outcasts out of Graceland? What do you or your reflection group think about the attitudes and behaviors of the Incasts toward the Outcasts? Later on in the biblical drama, what motivates the Outcasts to save the Incasts? What do you or your reflection group think about the attitudes and behaviors of the Outcasts toward the Incasts at the end of the biblical drama?

7. How do you or your reflection group believe the following qualities in people can promote and nurture human and religious freedom? The qualities are:
   (a) The gift of hospitality.
   (b) Learning to treasure your questions.
   (c) Remembering the wisdom and truth found in stories.
   (d) Seeking and finding value in what others discard.
   (e) Vulnerability that unlocks compassion in the heart.
   (f) Respect for the needs of the many.
   (g) Courage and hope in the face of obstacles.
   (h) Childlike enthusiasm, vision and zest for life.

8. In the "Prayer of St. Francis" we are invited into a world of paradox. What is a paradox? Have you or your reflection group experienced any paradoxes in your life? Explain. If you haven't, do you know of family or friends who have experienced paradoxes in their lives? In this prayer we are invited into a world where "it is in giving that we receive; it is in forgiving others that we ourselves are forgiven; and it is in dying that we are born to eternal life." In the experience of Christian freedom we are also invited into this world of paradox. I invite you or your reflection group to consider and brainstorm on some of the ways Christian freedom is not "freedom from" (some action) but "freedom to" (some committed, faith-filled action).

4. Jesus' Transfiguration

(Mark 9:2–10)

And after six days Jesus took with him Peter and James and John, and led them up a high mountain apart by themselves; and he was transfigured before them, and his garments became glistening, intensely white, as no fuller on earth could bleach them. And there appeared to them Elijah with Moses; and they were talking to Jesus. And Peter said to Jesus, "Master, it is well that we are here; let us make three booths, one for you and one for Moses and one for Elijah." For he did not know what to say, for they were exceedingly afraid. And a cloud over-shadowed them, and a voice came out of the cloud, "This is my beloved Son; listen to him." And suddenly looking around they no longer saw any one with them but Jesus only.

What On Earth Does It Mean?

CAST

Planner-1	Host
Planner-2	Contestant-1
Planner-3	Contestant-2
Student-1	Contestant-3
Student-2	Voice-1
Student-3	Voice-2
Teacher	Priest
Friend	Coach
Body-1	Body-2

SCENE ONE

[*Planner-1 and Planner-2 come into the acting area. They are carrying papers and books.*]

PLANNER-1:

We're missing Anne.

PLANNER-2:

She's late.

PLANNER-1:

What a revelation! Can you look into your crystal ball and tell me where she is?

PLANNER-2:
How should I know?

PLANNER-1:
Well you live in Dunne, don't you?

PLANNER-2:
Along with three hundred other people!

PLANNER-1:
She's always late and we've got a lot of work to do on this liturgy.

PLANNER-2:
Kevin, you sound like an anxiety attack waiting to burst into bloom. Relax! I know she'll be here any . . . (*Planner-2 sees Planner-3 coming toward them on crutches.*) Here she comes now.

PLANNER-3:
Sorry I'm late everybody. I've been running behind all day. And these crutches don't speed me up at all.

PLANNER-1:
Oh, that's ok.

PLANNER-2:
Lent must bring out the magnanimous part of you, Kevin. We might as well start planning this liturgy.

PLANNER-1:
Have you looked at those readings? The sacrifice of Isaac and the transfiguration? Talk about striking out!

PLANNER-2:
They must have some meaning. They must have something to say to us.

PLANNER-3:

Not necessarily! Remember, it's Lent. The church might be torturing us.

PLANNER-2:

I was struck by the image of the mountain. The sacrifice and the transfiguration took place on a mountain.

PLANNER-1:

So what do mountains remind you of?

PLANNER-2:

Getting away. In the midst of jammed days and fast-paced quarters, finding some way to get apart and get some perspective. If we never stop, look and listen, life is just a blur.

PLANNER-3:

I sure could use some of that. My days are becoming more and more rushed. And the worst part is that I always feel I'm behind and can't catch up. (*The Planners freeze and Scene Two begins.*)

SCENE TWO

STUDENT-1:

(*An alarm rings. Student-1 turns it off. It rings again and Student-1 turns it off again. Finally, it is so loud that she gets up and realizes she is late.*) Oh my God, I'm late again! (*Student-1 puts her watch on and keeps looking at it throughout the following encounters.*)

TEACHER:

Glad you could make it, Cari. Please see me in my office after class. That will be all for today. For next Monday remember that your reflection paper on *Hamlet* is due. Also finish reading *Much Ado About Nothing.* (*The class leaves. The*

Teacher goes to his office. Student-1 looks at her watch, hesitates, and then goes over to him.)

    Cari, you've got to be sharp in getting to my office. Either start getting to class on time or drop the class. It's as simple as that.

STUDENT-1:
I'll try, Professor Osorio.

TEACHER:
Try-ers are liars, Cari. Just be there! (*As Student-1 leaves, she runs into a Friend.*)

FRIEND:
You look terrible! I haven't seen you in ages.

STUDENT-1:
Why does everyone say that? I'm sorry, Paul. I've been meaning to call you. It's just that I've been so busy.

FRIEND:
Well, what about some lunch? You've got to eat.

STUDENT-1:
Today?

FRIEND:
Yes! I know this great little place down the Alameda.

STUDENT-1:
(*She looks at her watch.*) I'd love to, Paul, but I haven't got time. What about grabbing some fast food and talking on the way to the gym? (*Student-1 makes her way to the Coach.*)

COACH:
Cari, for God's sake where have you been?

STUDENT-1:
I've been running behind a bit.

COACH:

It's the second half already! And we've only got three people on the court.

STUDENT-1:

How are we doing?

COACH:

Don't ask. It's a massacre! Now get in there!

STUDENT-1:

(*She looks at her watch.*) I'm really sorry, Sean, but I've got a study group to go to. I can't miss it.

COACH:

O.K., Cari, but in the future let me know ahead of time. And get a substitute! (*Student-1 joins her study partners.*)

STUDENT-2:

What I can't figure out with Hamlet is why he can't make up his mind.

STUDENT-3:

But he does finally make up his mind to do something, to set his house in order.

STUDENT-2:

But it takes him half of the play.

STUDENT-1:

(*Cari looks at her watch.*) I'm sorry. I just can't concentrate. Could I get the notes from you later? (*Student-2 and Student-3 indicate "Yes."*)

I need to clear my head. I think I'll wander over to the evening liturgy. (*She joins the other members of this vignette who have become the congregation. They work together. The Priest leads them.*)

PRIEST:

> Praise the Lord.

ALL:

> Praise the Lord.

PRIEST:

> A quick reflection on the gospel. (*They all go into the thinker's position. They stand for the next prayer.*)
> Our Father . . . or Mother.

ALL:

> Our Father . . . or Mother.

PRIEST:

> Thanks be to God.

ALL:

> Thanks be to God.

PRIEST:

> Now get out of here! (*They all hurry to different parts of the church. Student-1 goes back to her room to sleep.*)

STUDENT-1:

> Long day. I've got to start slowing down. I've got to start smelling the roses. Oh well, tomorrow is another day.

SCENE THREE

PLANNER-1:

> Let's not forget that we're in the season of Lent. Perhaps that can bring out other dimensions of the readings.

PLANNER-2:

> Maybe that's where the idea of "sacrifice" comes in.

PLANNER-3:

Oh, that's great! What on earth does "sacrifice" mean?

PLANNER-2:

It can mean different things for different people.

PLANNER-3:

Please, don't even remind me. I haven't had time to come up with any lenten projects.

PLANNER-1:

What if Lent isn't about doing something more? What if it's about doing less?

PLANNER-3:

Well I haven't even had time to think of something I could give up.

PLANNER-2:

What about crazy paces and the unhealthy ways we treat ourselves and others? (*They ponder this and freeze.*)

SCENE FOUR

[*During this vignette, Body-1 is carrying Body-2 around. Body-2 hangs from his neck. She becomes heavier and heavier until she falls to the ground. There are two other characters that follow Body-1. Voice-1 is the Voice of Doubt. Voice-2 is the Voice of Reassurance.*]

VOICE-1:

There's your study partner, Dave. You've missed your last five meetings with Garth. There is no way on God's green earth that you are going to pass that organic chemistry final!

VOICE-2:

Don't listen to him, Dave. Garth will understand. And there's still time, if you set your mind to it now.

BODY-2:

Stop. Look. Listen.

VOICE-1:

Still haven't written that "thank you" note to Aunt Michele, have you? Well, pal, no more free lunches for you. You'll never see another penny from her at Christmas again!

VOICE-2:

You know your aunt will love you whether she hears from you or not. It's never too late to write and say "thank you."

BODY-2:

Stop. Look. Listen.

VOICE-1:

Your roommate has just about had it with you, Dave. You never pick up after yourself. Your side of the room is quickly becoming a stockpile of nuclear waste. Don't be surprised if you have to find a new roommate next year!

VOICE-2:

You can always say you're sorry, Dave, and start again. It won't take much to bring a little order to your chaos.

BODY-2:

Stop. Look. Listen.

VOICE-1:

There's Father Roche. You promised him you'd go on the senior retreat. You bailed out again, Dave. You score a big fat ZERO on the believability scale.

VOICE-2:

Just talk to him, Dave. He can understand being overextended and stressed out.

BODY-2:

Stop. Look. Listen. (*Body-2 collapses on the floor. Body-1 is visibly upset.*)

BODY-1:

Oh great. Just great! How can you do this to me? There are only two weeks left in the quarter. I'll slow down after finals. But you can't break down on me now. Not now! I count on you. Don't let me down!

BODY-2:

Stop. Look. Listen.

BODY-1:

But I don't have time to stop, look and listen!

BODY-2:

And how can you do this to me? (*They freeze.*)

SCENE FIVE

PLANNER-1:

I still don't see what all of this has to do with our being "People of the Promise."

PLANNER-3:

What promise?

PLANNER-2:

God promises to bless Abraham and his descendants abundantly. God promises to be with us always: in sickness, in health, through successes, through failures, in the good times and the difficult ones.

PLANNER-3:

I'm confused.

PLANNER-1:

I think you would be in good company.

PLANNER-3:

What do you mean?

PLANNER-1:

Look at Isaac and Abraham on that mountain of sacrifice. Look at Peter, James and John on the mountain of trans- figuration. Just think of the disciples as they will soon expe- rience their Teacher arrested, persecuted and finally put to death when they come down from that mountain and head for Jerusalem.

PLANNER-3:

But what on earth does it mean?

PLANNER-2:

I think it might mean, *on earth,* that God is found in those challenging and confusing experiences of our life if we don't run away from them.

PLANNER-1:

Maybe being "People of the Promise" involves something on our part.

PLANNER-3:

Like what?

PLANNER-2:

Like facing all those experiences in life that simply confuse and frighten us. Maybe that's the way we transform what we think are life's curses into life's blessings. (*All ponder this and freeze.*)

SCENE SIX

[*This vignette involves a play on the game show "Jeopardy." There are three contestants. One young man and one young woman are "All American" in visual presentation. They cannot, however, name any of life's challenging or confusing experiences. The third contestant is in a wheelchair. He is thoughtful and reflective. He always speaks last but correctly.*]

HOST:

A reminder, contestants, there are three minutes left in this Double Jeopardy round. Our current champion, Michele, hasn't gotten on the scoreboard yet. Garth, too, has a big goose egg under his name. And Eric is currently in the lead with $13,500. Eric, it's your turn again to choose a category.

CONTESTANT-3:

I'll try "Issues of Compassion" for $800.

HOST:

"A group of people subsidized by the Federal Government for periods of time, they are often unfairly characterized as 'lazy' and 'unwilling to work.'" (*Contestant-2 sounds her buzzer.*)

Michele.

CONTESTANT-2:

Who are graduates of Loyola-Marymount?

HOST:

I'm sorry. That's incorrect. (*Contestant-1 sounds his buzzer.*)

Garth.

CONTESTANT-1:

What are minorities?

HOST:

No. (*Contestant-3 sounds his buzzer.*)

Eric.

CONTESTANT-3:
Who are welfare recipients?

HOST:
That's correct. Select a category.

CONTESTANT-3:
"Health" for $600.

HOST:
"A relatively new disease, it is considered by many as devastating to the 20th century as the Black Plague was to the 14th century. It cannot be transmitted by casual touch or contact. To date there is no known cure for it." (*Contestant-1 sounds his buzzer.*)
Garth.

CONTESTANT-1:
What is Television Evangelism?

HOST:
No. (*Contestant-2 sounds her buzzer.*)
Michele.

CONTESTANT-2:
What is "bad taste in clothes?"

HOST:
Wrong. (*Contestant-3 sounds his buzzer.*)
Eric.

CONTESTANT-3:
What is Acquired Immune Deficiency Syndrome or AIDS?

HOST:
Absolutely correct! Select another category.

CONTESTANT-3:
I'll try "Issues of Compassion" for $1000.

HOST:

"Their situation has been characterized as the scandal of the 'American Dream.' The greatest percentage of them are single mothers and children. They have difficulty finding employment because they have no permanent address." (*Contestant-1 sounds his buzzer.*)
Garth.

CONTESTANT-1:

Who are former Playmates of the Month?

HOST:

That's incorrect. I'll just remind you, contestants, that our category is "Issues of Compassion." (*Contestant-2 sounds her buzzer.*)
Michele.

CONTESTANT-2:

Who are Grateful Dead Groupies?

HOST:

Wrong again. (*Contestant-3 sounds his buzzer.*)
Eric.

CONTESTANT-3:

Who are the homeless?

HOST:

That's right! Select again, please.

CONTESTANT-3:

I'll try "Beginnings and Endings" for $1000.

HOST:

"Elisabeth Kübler-Ross, in her now famous book on the subject, describes its successive stages as: anger, denial, bargaining, despair, and finally, acceptance." (*Contestant-2 sounds her buzzer first.*)
Michele.

CONTESTANT-2:

What are Presidential Primaries?

HOST:

I'm sorry. That's incorrect. (*Contestant-1 sounds his buzzer.*)
Garth.

CONTESTANT-1:

What are parental reactions to raises in tuition?

HOST:

Incorrect. (*Contestant-3 sounds his buzzer.*)
Eric.

CONTESTANT-3:

What is death?

HOST:

Absolutely right again! (*Buzzer sounds.*)

Alright, contestants, that indicates we are ready for our final Jeopardy question. The category is: Seasons. Put down your Final Jeopardy wager. Here is the answer:

"Considered a time of 'conversion,' this period of preparation comes before the great Christian feast. Prayer, fasting and almsgiving have been traditional ways of observing it."

You've got fifteen seconds to come up with the correct question. (*Here the entire cast hums the tune for final Jeopardy.*)
We'll start with Garth.

CONTESTANT-1:

What is "Only twenty more shopping days before Christmas?"

HOST:

Very consistent, Garth, but unfortunately wrong again. We'll move now to Michele. Your answer in the form of a question is?

CONTESTANT-2:

I was stumped. I put down "What is membership in Weight Watchers?"

HOST:

I'm sorry, Michele, that's incorrect. And Eric, our current leader, how did you respond?

CONTESTANT-3:

What is . . .

CONTESTANT-1:

(*Looks frustrated and intense.*) Miss it! (*All the characters freeze.*)

SCENE SEVEN

PLANNER-3:

The more we look and the more we reflect, the more we find.

PLANNER-1:

The amazing thing is that we're just starting to uncover what's there.

PLANNER-2:

Well, there's no way to exhaust a mystery. So let's not start putting up tents and trying to stay here forever. It didn't work back then and it won't work now.

PLANNER-3:

But what shape is all of this going to take in the liturgy? What are we going to share with them? I'm worried. We haven't come up with any answers.

PLANNER-1:

I leave most of the answers I hear in church right there. Questions, especially haunting questions, follow me through the entire week.

PLANNER-2:

Then let's share our questions with them. Let's invite them to ask their own questions.

PLANNER-3:

What kind of questions?

PLANNER-1:

The kind of questions they can ask every week and never completely exhaust the answer because it's a mystery.

PLANNER-3:

Questions about what?

PLANNER-2:

Questions about where God is found in the challenging and confusing parts of our lives.

PLANNER-1:

Questions like "Who are the poor?" "Who are the homeless?" "What is death?"

PLANNER-2:

Questions that, in one form or another, ask your question: "What on earth does it mean?"

Finis

PROPS

1. One small bench that can be used in Scene Two for the classroom and as a pew later in that same scene.
2. Books and Papers that can be used by Student-2 and Student-3 in Scene Two when they are a study group.
3. One clerical shirt or liturgical vestment to be worn by the Priest in Scene Two.
4. Three bar stools that can be used as contestant podiums in Scene Six.

PRODUCTION NOTES

This biblical dramatization was originally performed as a dramatized homily in a liturgy for the Second Sunday in Lent. Campus Ministry at Santa Clara University had organized a series of thematic celebrations that Lent entitled "People of the Promise." The references to both Lent and the "People of the Promise" series will make no sense at all to your congregation or audience unless the dramatization takes place during Lent and under the umbrella theme of "People of the Promise."

This is another example of how you will need to adapt these biblical dramas to your own pastoral occasion and needs. Other local references (Dunne Residence Hall) and Jesuit references (Loyola Marymount) will also need to be dropped or changed.

Certain characters are referred to by name (e.g., Paul, Cari, etc.). These were the names of the Biblical Explorers who first played these parts. It was easier for them, given the short amount of time we had to practice these dramas, to use their own names rather than memorize some fictitious name. I strongly encourage you to adapt the script and use the names of the people working with you.

Occasionally choices are made in these biblical dramatizations for their symbolic significance. An example of that can be seen in Scene Four. I chose to have a young man play the part of Body-1 and a young woman play the part of Body-2. Why? I was symbolizing attitudes and behaviors here. The attitudes and behaviors of Body-1 are what I would designate "masculine" in a Jungian sense. The attitudes, behaviors and, ultimately, wisdom of Body-2 are what I would designate "feminine" in a similar Jungian sense.

Whether you agree or disagree with my designations, you may ask another significant question: "Will the people who watch this biblical dramatization pick up the significance of these choices and this symbolism?" I don't think symbolism works on people consciously. I believe it works on our subconscious or unconscious. To have the visual presentation of the attitudes and behaviors of Body-1 as a man and to have the visual presentation of the attitudes and behaviors of Body-2 as a woman may work on your congregation's or audience's subconscious. They may begin reflecting on the symbolic meaning of all of this by asking the simple and obvious question: "Why did that guy have that girl hanging around his neck?" If they refer this question to you, please don't answer it for them. Like Jesus and many other superb teachers, invite them to explore their own questions. Just smile and say: "That's a very good question. Why do you think that guy had a girl hanging around his neck?"

Another significant choice, in this biblical dramatization, was to have Contestant-3 seated in a wheelchair. Too often people with physical disabilities are totally dismissed. I think a person in a wheelchair is a powerful symbol. Suffering can potentially give birth to compassion and wisdom in those who are open to being transformed by their suffering. The wheelchair became a symbol of all those "differently-abled" than us, whom we all too often write off. It is this person (i.e., the symbolic image of the classic fool, the person easily overlooked or disregarded) who really has the knowledge, the truth, the compassion and wisdom we so desperately need for survival on this planet. If people are conscious of the significance of this choice, all the better. If not, let the visual image work on them subconsciously and lead them to potentially life-giving questions.

In this dramatization, as in others, the entire ensemble made sound effects when they were called for. As the contestants slammed their hands on the top of their bar stools, the cast would make a loud "buzzer" sound. During the "Final Jeopardy" part of Scene Six, when the cast began humming the tune played on the television version of this show, the whole congregation joined in the humming.

REFLECTION QUESTIONS AND EXERCISES

1. Mark's account of this incident is both very dramatic and very sketchy. He leaves a great deal to our imaginations. I invite you or your reflection group to read this miracle story from Mark's gospel (Mk 9:2–10), and pay special attention to the conversations that take place in this story. We can be changed by conversations we are part of or conversations we overhear. Jesus

is seen talking with Moses and Elijah. Who was Moses? What does he symbolize or represent for the Israelites? Who was Elijah? What does he symbolize or represent for the Israelites? What do you think is the significance of Jesus speaking with Moses and Elijah? What in the world do you think they were talking about?

Peter talks with Jesus. Somewhat awed by what he and the disciples are seeing, Peter suggests building three tents or booths on the mountain. Why do you think Peter suggests doing this? What do the tents or booths symbolize?

A Voice is heard from the cloud speaking to the disciples about Jesus. What does the Voice say? Where is this affirmation coming from? If you had been one of the disciples and heard this, what would you think? How well would you "listen" to this person after such an experience?

Jesus tells the disciples not to tell anyone about what happened. Why do you think Jesus tells them this? If you had been one of the disciples, would you have been able to keep this experience a secret? Why or why not? Explain.

Although it is not recorded, the disciples surely must have talked about the event with each other. What do you think they said to one another? Remember that only Peter, James and John went with Jesus and experienced this. If you had been one of the disciples who had not gone along and experienced these events, and you heard one of the three who talked about these extraordinarily puzzling events, what would your reaction have been?

2. In this biblical story from Mark's gospel, Jesus is changed before his disciples. I invite you or your reflection group to consider some of life's experiences that change us and the way we look at things.

How have you or your reflection group changed physically? How have these physical changes affected you? Has growing up or growing older changed you or people you know and love? How has this changed you or them? Have you ever spent time in a hospital, a cast or a wheelchair? If you haven't, do you know of anyone who has? How have these changes affected you or them? Have you ever experienced psychological changes, attitudinal changes or emotional swings? How have these changes affected you? How has your spirituality (i.e., your relationship with God) changed? How have these changes affected your faith, your attitudes and behaviors? Explain. Have you noticed any changes in your values? Why or why not? Explain.

How have you experienced "birth" or "new life" in your life? Experiences of birth and new life can change us. How have these experiences changed you? What did you come to know or experience through these births that you had not known or experienced before? Experiences of loss and death can change us. Have you or your reflection group experienced loss through the death of a parent, a spouse, a child or close friend? How have these losses changed you? What did you come to know or experience through these painful experiences of loss that you had not known or experienced before?

Looking back over your life, what little changes have transfigured and transformed your life? How have they done this? What changes in your life have forced you to reexamine and sometimes change your priorities?

3. In the biblical story, mountains are usual settings for supernatural revelations and theophanies. Mountains become a symbol of the God-experience. I invite you or your reflection group to consider the ways you have experienced the presence of God in your life.

First of all, who have been one or two of the God-persons in your life? By "God-person" I mean someone who quite unselfconsciously revealed the presence or love of God to you by some quality or characteristic of their attitude and behavior. What was it about them that made them a God-person for you? How did these persons change you? Explain. If you do this in your reflection group, slowly go around your faith-sharing circle and allow people to tell the stories of their God-persons.

Secondly, what have been God-places in your life? Where have you experienced the presence and love of God? What was it about these places that made them God-places for you? An Hasidic story about the dwelling places of God has a Rabbi answer the question: "Where does God dwell?" with the reply: "Wherever we let God in." What do you or your reflection group think about the possible wisdom and truth of the Rabbi's words? Explain. How did these God-places change you? Explain.

Thirdly, what have been God-experiences in your life? I doubt whether we will all have such a dramatic experience as Peter, James and John on the Mountain of Transfiguration, but we will have experiences of God's presence and love that will mold us and mark us and change us. Looking back on your life, what have been some of those experiences for you? How did these experiences reveal God's presence or love to you? How did these experiences change you? Explain.

4. In Scene Two of the biblical dramatization, Student-1 is running everywhere. She is always late. Her life seems out of control. Have you ever felt as if your life were "out of control?" Why or why not? Explain. When you experience times like this, how do you find perspective? What experiences put things in perspective for you or your reflection group? What is there about such experiences that help to give us some needed balance and healthy perspective? Explain.

I would like you or your reflection group to reflect on the following experiences. Have you personally experienced any of them? If so, have they helped give you needed perspective in your life? Why or why not? Explain. Here is the list of experiences:

(a) Illness.
(b) A twenty-first birthday.
(c) Active involvement in a community service organization.
(d) Depression.
(e) Death.
(f) Distance.
(g) Time.
(h) A retreat.
(i) Reading a certain book.
(j) Traveling.

Have you ever gotten perspective by spending some time in a "safe place"? What does a "safe place" symbolize for you? What qualities or characteristics does a "safe place" possess? Where do you find those "safe places" in your life?

5. The following exercise is geared to help you take a good look at what a balanced life might look like. It also invites you to imagine changes you could make in the way you actually live your life right now, if you don't find your life is as balanced as you would like it to be. You will need some paper and a pencil or pen for each person doing this exercise.

Draw two circles or pies next to each other on the front of your piece of paper. Divide the first pie into fourths (four equal wedges). Label the wedges: (a) work, (b) play, (c) prayer/reflection, and (d) relationships. Now divide the second pie into four wedges (named above) whose size would indicate the actual amount of time per week you spend engaged in them. This pie should represent the amount of time you spend each week with these four different aspects of your life. Is the pie that reflects your lived life balanced? Why or why not? Would you like to change the size of any of these wedges? What would you have to do in order to change them?

Now take another piece of paper. Divide it into four equal parts. Draw a picture of yourself at work. Draw a picture of yourself at play. Draw a picture of yourself at prayer or reflecting. Draw a picture of yourself in relationships. Don't say you can't draw. Make stick figures. Do something visual on that piece of paper that somehow captures how you see yourself (a) at work, (b) at play, (c) at prayer or reflection, and (d) in relationships. When everyone in the group has had a chance to do their drawings, have each person in the group share with the others their drawing of themselves at work. Share with the group what aspects, conflicts or frustrations of yourself at work this picture captures. Now repeat this process with the other three categories.

After everyone has had an opportunity to share their pictures and stories, ask each person to select one of those pictures and aspects of their life that they would like to change. What would you like to change about this picture? What would you need to do in order to change it? Draw a picture of yourself in this aspect of your life the way you would like it to be.

6. What does "sacrifice" mean to you or your reflection group? Who has sacrificed for us in our life? What have they sacrificed? Who or what would you be willing to sacrifice for in your

life? What would you be willing to sacrifice in order to achieve a cherished goal or in order to accomplish a desired end?

What are some of the unhealthy ways we treat ourselves and others? What attitudes (conscious or unconscious) lie behind such behaviors? How would you go about changing destructive or unhealthy attitudes and behaviors?

Scene Four of the biblical dramatization introduces us to voices of doubt and voices of reassurance. Have you ever experienced voices of doubt in your life? Why or why not? Explain. If so, what did those voices of doubt say to you? Have you ever experienced voices of assurance in your life? Why or why not? Explain. If so, what did those voices of assurance say to you? Which voices are easier to listen to? Why is it easier to listen to these voices?

7. In Scene Four of this biblical dramatization, Body-1 carries Body-2 who is hanging around his neck. What do you or your reflection group think this represents? Why does Body-2 keep saying: "Stop. Look. Listen." What are some of the ways that you or your reflection group "Stop" in your everyday life? Explain. What are some of the ways that you or your reflection group "Look" in your everyday life? Explain. What are some of the ways that you or your reflection group "Listen" in your everyday life? Explain.

Leo Rock, author of *Making Friends with Yourself* (New Jersey: Paulist Press, 1990) which I highly recommend to you for reading and reflection on this and other topics, once wrote me: "Whoever said: 'The unreflective life is not worth living' had half the truth. The other half: 'The unlived life is not worth reflecting.'" What do you or your reflection group think is meant by the phrase: "The unreflective life is not worth living"? Do you agree or disagree with this evaluation? Explain. What do you or your reflection group think Leo Rock means by the phrase: "The unlived life is not worth reflecting"? Do you agree or disagree with his evaluation? Explain.

8. Gerald of Wales, in his *The Journey Through Wales* (London: Penguin Classics, 1978), begins his reflections by saying: "God's ways are always just but not always easy to understand."

What do you or your reflection group think that Gerald means by this? Do you agree or disagree with his evaluation? Explain.

As a colleague of mine quipped: "Hindsight is always 20–20." In Scene Five of the biblical dramatization, Planner-2 says that God is found in those challenging and confusing experiences of our life if we don't run away from them. Do you or your reflection group agree or disagree with this evaluation? Explain.

What have been some of the more challenging experiences in your life? Looking back on them, how might God have been present in those challenges? Explain.

What have been some of the more confusing experiences in your life? Looking back on them, how might God have been present in that confusion? Explain.

In Scene Seven of this biblical drama, Planner-1 says: "Questions, especially haunting questions, follow me through the entire week." Do you or your reflection group agree or disagree with his evaluation? Explain. What are some of the "haunting questions" you have experienced in your life? Did these questions change you in any way? If so, how? If not, why not? Explain.

5. Healing the Sick

(Mark 5:21–43)

And when Jesus had crossed again in the boat to the other side, a great crowd gathered about him; and he was beside the sea. Then came one of the rulers of the synagogue, Jairus by name; and seeing him, he fell at his feet, and besought him, saying, "My little daughter is at the point of death. Come and lay your hands on her, so that she may be made well, and live." And he went with him.

And a great crowd followed him and thronged about him. And there was a woman who had had a flow of blood for twelve years, and who had suffered much under many physicians, and had spent all that she had, and was no better but rather grew worse. She had heard the reports about Jesus, and came up behind him in the crowd and touched his garment. For she said, "If I touch even his garments, I shall be made well." And immediately the hemorrhage ceased; and she felt in her body that she was healed of her disease. And Jesus, perceiving in himself that power had gone forth from him, immediately turned about in the crowd, and said, "Who touched my garments?" And his disciples said to him, "You see the crowd pressing around you, and yet you say, 'Who touched me?' " And he looked around to see who had done it. But the woman, knowing what had been done to her, came in fear and trembling and fell down before him, and told him the whole truth. And he said to her, "Daughter, your faith has made you well; go in peace, and be healed of your disease."

While he was still speaking, there came from the ruler's house some who said, "Your daughter is dead. Why trouble the Teacher any further?" But ignoring what they said, Jesus said to the ruler of the synagogue, "Do not fear, only believe." And he allowed no one to follow him except Peter and James and John the brother of James. When they came to the house of the ruler of the synagogue, he saw a tumult, and people weeping and wailing loudly. And when he had entered, he said to them, "Why do you make a tumult and weep? The child is not dead but sleeping." And they laughed at him. But he put them all outside, and took the child's father and mother and those who were with him, and went in where the child was. Taking her by the hand he said to her, "Talitha cumi"; which means, "Little girl, I say to you, arise." And immediately the girl got up and walked; for she was twelve years old. And immediately they were overcome with amazement. And he strictly charged them that no one should know this, and told them to give her something to eat.

What Is Needed Is Trust

CAST

Man	Self
Woman	Roomie
Animus	Counselor
Anima	Friend-1
Boy	Friend-2
Girl	Child-1
Chorus-1	Child-2
Chorus-2	Mom
Dad	

[**Note:** This dramatization consists of four scenes that do not logically follow one upon the other. They are four scenes connected by the unifying refrain: "Fear is useless. What is needed is trust." The dramatization begins with an ensemble tableau consisting of one action frozen from each of the four scenes. The actors then jointly proclaim: "Fear is useless. What is needed is trust." After a pause, all but the actors for the first scene leave the acting area.]

SCENE ONE

[*The Man comes into the room and sees the Woman. He is stunned by her beauty. They both freeze for a second. Then, Man's Animus and Anima begin working on him.*]

ANIMUS:

> She's looking at you. Try not to act like a nerd!

ANIMA:

> Be yourself.

ANIMUS:

> Look at yourself, you idiot. Who wears stripes and argyles at the same time? You better hope she's nearsighted. Honestly, where did you get that shopper's special? At K-Mart?

ANIMA:

> Be yourself.

ANIMUS:

> What a sorry excuse for a human being. What makes you think she'd even notice you? If your personality was compared to the annual rainfall of this valley, you'd be a drought! Lighten up, Frankenstein! Who wants to meet a mortician?

ANIMA:

> Be yourself.

ANIMUS:

> What's that in your hand? Darwin's *Survival of the Species*? Something to wrap her mind around? What a total turnoff!

ANIMA:

> Be yourself.

ANIMUS:

> What are those unsightly stains, Egghead? (*Man looks at his pants.*)
>
> No, higher, you imbecile! (*Animus begins to sniff and scrunch his face.*)
>
> What's that distinctive landfill aroma I'm wafting? Essence of Tidy Bowl?

ANIMA:

Be yourself.

ANIMUS:

How can such a wimpy body create such a big stink? Look at you. You're a wreck! Look at those legs. Stand on one of them and you'd be mistaken for a stork! Are those biceps or pimples on a bone? What a walking disaster! You qualify for emergency Federal funding!

ANIMA:

Be yourself.

ANIMUS:

Oh-oh, here she comes. Dum-da-dum-dum!

WOMAN:

Hi, I'm Chris. What's your name?

MAN:

I really don't know why I wear argyles with stripes. I'm not awake in the morning.

WOMAN:

I'm Chris. What's your name?

MAN:

I know I must seem dull but I'm really quite mediocre when you get to know me.

WOMAN:

What's that you're reading?

MAN:

What? (*Nervously tosses the book away.*)
Oh that? I don't know where that came from. I don't even know how to read!

WOMAN:

What's your name?

MAN:

Do you smell something? I must have stepped in something! I know that my quads, glutes and pects are in a dormant stage but I'm working on 'em!

WOMAN:

What's your name?

MAN:

My name. Yes, what is my name? I have a name. Just a minute. (*Man looks in his wallet.*)

Todd. Yes. Yes. That's it! Todd's my name.

WOMAN:

Hi Todd, I'm Chris. Where are you from? (*They begin to walk off. All freeze. All the other actors proclaim: "Fear is useless. What is needed is trust." The members of Scene Two come into the acting area.*)

SCENE TWO

SELF:

Hi, Laura.

ROOMIE:

Hi, Tricia. What's up?

SELF:

Ah, nothing much. (*Self communicates lethargy bordering on depression through her tone of voice.*)

ROOMIE:

Come on, now. What's wrong with you? You can't hide it from your old roommate. Now what's bothering you?

SELF:
It's my younger brother, who was killed in the car accident six months ago. I can't stop thinking about him. I can't get him out of my head. I really miss him.

ROOMIE:
Tricia, I know exactly what you're feeling. (*Nodding her head reassuringly.*)

SELF:
You do?

ROOMIE:
Yes. I remember when my hamster died. I thought I'd never stop crying. But you'll get over it. I did! My mother got me a new one the next week.

SELF:
I don't think my mother can do that for me.

ROOMIE:
If you dwell on it, it's just going to make things worse. (*Exasperated.*)
Maybe you should see a counselor. (*The Roomie freezes as Self moves to the Counselor.*)

SELF:
(*To Counselor.*) But when am I going to get over it?

COUNSELOR:
Trish, I don't think we ever get over the death of one we love. They're not a hamster we can replace.

SELF:
So what do I do?

COUNSELOR:
Exactly what you're doing. You talk about it. You remember. It takes time, Trish, lots of time. But it's healing.

SELF:

But who will listen?

COUNSELOR:

I will. And your friends will too.

SELF:

It'll just be a downer.

COUNSELOR:

Some of your friends will be frightened and run away. Others will be afraid. They won't know what to say or do. But they'll stay and face those fears. They'll listen to you. (*Counselor freezes. Self moves to Friends.*)

FRIEND-1:

He was what?

SELF:

Killed.

FRIEND-2:

How?

SELF:

Car accident.

FRIEND-1:

When?

SELF:

Six months ago.

FRIEND-2:

Oh Trish! (*Friend-2 embraces Trish. Friend-1 reaches out and puts his hand on her shoulder. All freeze as the other actors say: "Fear is useless. What is needed is trust." After a brief pause, the players from Scene Two leave and the players for Scene Three move into the acting area.*)

SCENE THREE

BOY:

Hi, Chrissie. How's it going?

GIRL:

Great! How about you, Garth?

BOY:

I've been busy. Seems like we have a chem midterm every day.

GIRL:

I know what you mean. Look at me. My roomie's basking in the Mission Gardens, while I'm rotting in Orradre.

BOY:

The pace is too intense. I'm afraid I'll fry my brain.

GIRL:

We're stressing "Big Time."

BOY:

We need a break.

GIRL:

There's the Boat Dance this weekend. Are you going?

BOY:

I don't know. I've got an exam. What about you?

GIRL:

Well, nobody's asked me yet.

BOY:

Chrissie, there's someting I've been meaning to tell you.

GIRL:

What, Garth?

BOY:

Well, I kinda, I mean I sorta, . . . Chrissie, I like you a lot. You're a lot of fun to be with and I'm really attracted to you.

GIRL:

I'm scared, Garth.

BOY:

I'm scared too.

GIRL:

What will this do to our friendship? (*They turn their backs to one another and freeze. Chorus-1 and Chorus-2 come up to the Boy and Girl and begin their haunting set of accusatory questions. The other actors begin echoing the questions and Chorus voices.*)

CHORUS-1:

(*To the Boy.*) What did you say?

CHORUS-2:

(*To the Girl.*) What did you say?

CHORUS-1:

(*To the Boy.*) You blew it!

CHORUS-2:

(*To the Girl.*) You blew it!

CHORUS-1:

(*To the Boy.*) What are you going to do now?

CHORUS-2:

(*To the Girl.*) What are you going to do now?

CHORUS-1:

(*To the Boy.*) She's right behind you.

CHORUS-2:
> (*To the Girl.*) He's right behind you.

CHORUS-1:
> (*To the Boy.*) What's taking so long?

CHORUS-2:
> (*To the Girl.*) What's taking so long?

BOY:
> (*Together with Girl.*) ENOUGH!

GIRL:
> (*Together with Boy.*) ENOUGH! (*They face one another and freeze. The actors offstage say: "Fear is useless. What is needed is trust." After a pause, the players from Scene Three leave and are replaced by the players from Scene Four.*)

SCENE FOUR

CHILD-1:
> Good-bye, Mom. (*They hug.*)

CHILD-2:
> Good-bye, Dad. (*They start to hug, then shake hands.*)

MOM:
> Be sure and write.

CHILD-1:
> Oh Mom, we heard the jingle: "Reach out! Reach out and touch someone."

DAD:
> Remember: don't do anything that I wouldn't do! (*Forced nerd laugh!*)

MOM:

What a kidder! Now boys, remember this: whenever you're going out, always wear clean underwear!

CHILD-2:

O.K., O.K., Mom.

DAD:

(*Putting arms around both children as they move toward the door.*) Now this is a little something to tide you over in case of emergencies.

CHILD-1:

Thanks, Dad.

CHILD-2:

See you in June! (*All the characters freeze. A Chorus figure comes on and indicates the passage of time.*)

CHORUS-1:

Nine months later. (*Child-2 moves offstage. Child-1 returns home to greet Mom and Dad.*)

CHILD-1:

Hi Mom! Hi Dad!

MOM:

Welcome home!

DAD:

Good to see you. You've really changed.

CHILD-1:

Yeah, college does that to you. Greg's changed too. Have you talked to him?

MOM:

About what?

DAD:

Yes, son, about what?!!

CHILD-1:

Oh nothing. I'm sure he'd want to tell you in person. (*There is an awkward pause. They freeze. Child-2 comes bursting onto the scene.*)

CHILD-2:

Hey Mom! (*He goes to embrace her and she is awkward.*)

Hi Dad! (*He goes to embrace Dad and Dad holds out his hand for a handshake. They all sit down. There's a period of awkward silence.*)

So, how are things around here?

MOM:

Fine, son. Just fine.

DAD:

How about you?

CHILD-1:

Say, did you get my sleeping bag out of the car?

CHILD-2:

No.

CHILD-1:

Well, I think I'll just haul my stuff up to my room and settle in. (*Child-1 leaves at this point.*)

DAD:

So how was school?

MOM:

I'll bet you're starving after that long drive. Your father has been working over a hot stove all day just to fix you boys something to eat. If you'll excuse me, I'll check on that food and make sure nothing is burning. (*Mom leaves the stage area.*)

DAD:

So, how was school?

CHILD-2:

It was good. I learned a lot.

DAD:

You did? About what?

CHILD-2:

Oh, about a lot of things.

DAD:

Like what?

CHILD-2:

Like myself.

DAD:

You know something, your mother's been gone for a long time. I better go see if everything is O.K. (*Dad leaves the acting area. There is an awkward and long pause.*)

CHILD-2:

Mom, Dad, I'm glad we have this chance to talk. There's something I've been wanting to tell you for a long time . . . (*Child-2 freezes. After a pause, the Chorus says: "Fear is useless. What is needed is trust." After a few moments of silence, the lights slowly come down and the players leave.*)

Finis

PROPS

1. One book for the Man in Scene One.
2. One wallet for the Man in Scene One.
3. Five bar stools or their equivalents for Scene Two. Two of the bar stools will be set up for the interaction between Self and

Counselor. Three of the bar stools will be set up for the interaction between Self and the two Friends.
4. Two small suitcases or dufflebags for Scene Four.
5. One sleeping bag for Scene Four.
6. One small bench for Scene Four. Child-2 can sit on it for his
last lines.

PRODUCTION NOTES

This biblical dramatization calls for very little in the way
of props. You do not have to use any of the props suggested. It
demonstrates how your group can perform such a drama in a
simple and uncomplicated manner.

At the risk of stating the obvious, let me remind you that
if you are using this biblical dramatization as a catechetical resource, be sure and adapt it to your needs. It would probably be
more desirable, in a catechetical setting, to use only one of the
scenes of this biblical dramatization and to use it as a "jumping
board" into further reflection and discussion.

Hopefully the experience of the dramatization itself, as well
as exploring some of the reflection questions and exercises, will
suggest other imaginative possibilities to you and your class or
reflection group. Do not allow either the biblical dramatization
or its reflection material to become a straightjacket. You and
your group may discover imaginative connections that we simply could not and did not envision. Dynamic faith-sharing for
you and your reflection group will lie precisely in exploring
those newly discovered connections.

REFLECTION QUESTIONS AND EXERCISES

1. St. Ignatius of Loyola in the *Spiritual Exercises* encourages
those contemplating biblical scenes to imaginatively put themselves into the biblical story (No. 114, 115, 116, etc.). I invite you
or your reflection group to explore this biblical story in precisely
this way. I also invite you to do it in a variety of ways. First,

imagine that you are one of the privileged disciples (Peter, James and John) who accompanied Jesus. What do you hear as you move through these two miracle stories (i.e., the raising of Jairus' daughter and the healing of the woman with the hemorrhage)? What action do you witness? What do you think, feel and physically sense as you move through these stories?

Go into the biblical story a second time as a servant or friend of Jairus. What do you hear the characters say? What do you see them do? How do these actions and words affect you? What do you think, feel and physically sense as you move through these biblical stories?

Go into the biblical story a third time as the woman with the hemorrhage or a very close friend or relative that has accompanied her. What do you hear the characters say? What do you see the characters do? How do these actions and words affect you? What do you think, feel and physically sense as you move through these biblical stories?

What do you or the members of your reflection group learn about the person of Christ through your experience and observations as a disciple? What do you or the members of your reflection group learn about the person of Christ as Jairus or one of his servants or friends? What do you or the members of your reflection group learn about the person of Christ as the woman with the hemorrhage or one of the people who accompanies her?

2. In the healing of the woman with the hemorrhage, we read that when she touched him Jesus felt "power going out of him" (Mk 5:30). Any misunderstanding that this "power" is magical is quickly corrected by the following verses which show that faith is a necessary disposition for genuine healing to occur (see the *Jerome Biblical Commentary,* New Jersey: Prentice-Hall, Inc., 1968, "The Gospel According to Mark" by Edward J. Mally, S.J.).

I invite you or your reflection group to consider some of the experiences you may have had of power going out from you. How might the following experiences be aspects of power going out from you?

(a) A rock star or popular rock groups, sports figures, people in high public office or presidential candidates: Why do people want to be near them or touch them? Do people experience power coming out of them? Why or why not? Explain.

(b) Credit card and bank cards: Do you experience power coming out of them? Do they give you the power to buy anything you want? If so, is that power helpful or harmful? Explain. If not, why not? Explain.

(c) Blood transfusions: If you have ever donated blood, could that be an experience of power coming out of you? Why or why not? Explain.

(d) Artists, creative and imaginative people: What type of power comes out of artists' creativity and imagination? Explain.

(e) Doctors or surgeons: Have you ever dealt with them and felt power coming out of them? Was this power helpful or harmful? Explain.

(f) Knowledge as power: Have you ever prepared for an exam or a talk you had to give or a paper you had to present, and when you took it or gave it experienced power coming out from you? In what ways is knowledge powerful? Can knowledge be helpful and harmful? Why or why not? Explain

(g) Words of rejection, ridicule or abuse: How has power come out of you when you have uttered or experienced these kinds of words? Explain.

(h) Words of praise, affirmation or acceptance: How has power come out of you when you have uttered or experienced these kinds of words? Explain.

(i) What other human experiences can you or your reflection group think of that could be described as power coming out of you?

3. For the following imaginative exercise, you or the reflection group will need a piece of paper and a pencil or pen. In the biblical story about the raising of Jairus' daughter, Jesus tells Jairus that "Fear is useless. What is needed is trust." What do you or your reflection group think Jesus meant by these words? Is there truth or wisdom in these words? Why or why not? Explain.

Do these words have any application (past, present or future) to you in the circumstances of your life? Why or why not? Explain.

I would like you or your reflection group to consider all of those experiences in your life that evoke fear in you. Simply ask yourself the question: "What frightens me?" or "What am I afraid of?" Write down the first thing that comes to mind. Then, ask yourself the question again. Keep doing this over and over until you are satisfied that you have named a number of the things (past, present or future) that evoke fear in you.

Now that you have this list of fears, I invite you or your reflection group to take turns in naming these fears. Each time a person names a fear, pause for a moment and then have the entire group proclaim Christ's words to Jairus: "Fear is useless. What is needed is trust."

After you have completed this exercise, I think it would be helpful to reflect and share with others what you experienced as you went through this. What impact (if any) did you experience when your fears were confronted with Christ's invitation to faith?

4. In the biblical story about the woman with the hemorrhage, we read that "she had spent all she had without being any the better for it." The means she took (i.e., her money and people to whom she went for help) did not achieve the end she desired (i.e., healing).

People in our society often take a tranquilizer to deal with anxiety rather than dealing directly with the causes of that anxiety. Increasingly people of our culture and society rely on alcohol and drugs to cope with the conflict and confusion they find in life. While these stimulants and depressants can anesthetize us for a few hours, when the effect wears off the problem and challenge is still there. In light of the above, I invite you or your reflection group to consider the following questions.

What are the ways in which our society is hemorrhaging? What are the causes of this hemorrhaging? What can we do to "stop the bleeding?" What are some of the ways we spend our resources to cure or heal this bleeding that simply do not work? What are some of the means that might work which we haven't tried? What keeps us from trying these?

What are the methods we try in order to make ourselves worthwhile, valuable, noticeable or attractive:

(a) work?

(b) the clothes we wear?

(c) the people we associate with?

(d) personality?

(e) a car or the kind of car we drive?

(f) money?

(g) position?

(h) power?

(i) self-image?

(j) hygiene (i.e., mouthwash, deodorant, perfume or cologne)?

(k) values?

(l) other things your group thinks of?

5. St. Irenaeus once said that "the glory of God is the human person fully alive." Discernment is the process whereby we select from all the possible choices we have the one we think will be the best. Christian discernment involves making the choice that we believe would help us be most "fully alive."

I invite you or your reflection group to reflect on decisions you have made in your life. How did you go about deciding which choice to make? What are some of the choices you have made in your life that have resulted in your feeling very much alive? Explain. What are some of the choices you have made in your life that appeared to be life-giving but did not or could not deliver? Explain.

St. Ignatius of Loyola has a very pragmatic yardstick for measuring good and bad discernments. First, can you live with the decisions you make? Second, what comes from the decisions you make (i.e., happiness and peace or agitation and regret)? What are some of the decisions you have made that you have been able to live with? Explain. What have you experienced as a result of those choices? Explain. What are some of the decisions you have not been able to live with? Explain. What did you experience as a result of those choices? Explain.

6. In Scene One and Scene Three characters are addressed by a number of Voices. These Voices that we see visualized in this biblical dramatization represent the voices that each of us hears inside ourselves. What are some of the Voices of Doubt that you hear in your life? Where do those Voices of Doubt come from? What shapes and expressions do those Voices of Doubt take in your life? Is it easy or difficult to listen to those Voices of Doubt? Explain.

What are the Voices of Affirmation that you hear in your life? Where do those Voices of Affirmation come from? What shapes and expressions do those Voices of Affirmation take in your life? Is it easy or difficult to listen to those Voices of Affirmation? Explain.

Which Voices (i.e., Voices of Doubt or Voices of Affirmation) lead you ultimately to becoming more "fully alive"? Explain.

7. In Scene Two, what do you or your reflection group think about the character Roomie's reaction to what's bothering Self? Is Roomie being sensitive or insensitive? How? Why? Explain.

What do you or your reflection group think about the Counselor's reaction to Self? Does the Counselor give Self good advice? Why or why not? Explain. Is the Counselor telling the truth? Why or why not? Explain. Is there any wisdom in the Counselor's words? Why or why not? Explain.

What do you or your reflection group think about the reaction of Friend-1 and Friend-2 to Self's situation? Are they being sensitive or insensitive? How? Why? Explain.

If one of your friends was experiencing what Self does in Scene Two, how would you respond? Would you be "frightened and run away"? Why or why not? Explain. Would you be "afraid, not know what to say but face those fears and stay to listen"? Why or why not? Explain.

8. In Scene Four, Child-1 tells his parents that Child-2 has changed. Have you ever gone away to school or left home for a period of time? Did you change in any significant ways as a result of this experience and time away? How did you change? How did your family and friends react to you when you returned?

Why do you or your reflection group think it is so hard for people to change? Explain. Why do you or your reflection group think it is so hard for people to accept changes in others? Explain.

How do you or your reflection group think Child-2 has changed? Explain. What do you think Child-2 wanted to tell his Mother and Father that they were afraid to hear? Explain.

6. The Feeding of the Five Thousand

(Matthew 14:13–21)

Now when Jesus heard this, he withdrew from there in a boat to a lonely place apart. But when the crowds heard it, they followed him on foot from the towns. As he went ashore he saw a great throng; and he had compassion on them, and healed their sick. When it was evening, the disciples came to him and said, "This is a lonely place, and the day is now over; send the crowds away to go into the villages and buy food for themselves." Jesus said, "They need not go away; you give them something to eat." They said to him, "We have only five loaves here

and two fish." And he said, "Bring them here to me."
Then he ordered the crowds to sit down on the grass; and
taking the five loaves and the two fish he looked up to
heaven, and blessed, and broke and gave the loaves to
the disciples, and the disciples gave them to the crowds.
And they all ate and were satisfied. And they took up
twelve baskets full of the broken pieces left over. And
those who ate were about five thousand men, besides
women and children.

Give Them Something to Eat

CAST

Bartender   Contestant-1
Customer-1   Contestant-2
Customer-2   Contestant-3
Customer-3   Dilemma-1
Narrator   Dilemma-2
Larry   Dilemma-3
Francine   Host
Helen   Steven
Sue   Danielle
Priest

SCENE ONE

[*The acting area is set up for the dramatization. Contestant-3 comes out and speaks.*]

CONTESTANT-3:

Give them something to eat. (*Contestant-3 then moves back with the congregation as the dramatists for Scene One come out. They set up three or four bar stools. This scene takes place in a bar. The bartender is cleaning glasses as the first person comes in.*)

BARTENDER:

Now what brings a nice girl like you into a dump like this?

CUSTOMER-1:
I can always count on you, Dave, to pick me up.

BARTENDER:
The usual?

CUSTOMER-1:
I can't take it anymore!

BARTENDER:
Then try a different drink.

CUSTOMER-1:
I'm not talking about drinks, Dave. I'm talking about life.

BARTENDER:
What's got you down?

CUSTOMER-1:
This has been the worst year of my life. First my mother dies. Then my husband's killed in an automobile accident. Yesterday I found out my best friend has cancer. It's just not fair.

BARTENDER:
Who said life is fair, kiddo?

CUSTOMER-1:
I just feel so alone right now. And the very people who would help me out of these funks are gone. My mother was a laugher. She could find humor in anything: young republicans, libertarians, stock market crashes. And my husband was constantly happy. He could always find good in people and events. He would always stress the positive.

BARTENDER:
Well, death can't take away your memories, kiddo. Somehow I believe that those we love leave us part of their spirit when they die. Maybe in a little time you'll rediscover a part

of your Mom's humor and your husband's positive outlook. (*With that Customer-2 comes in and demands a drink.*)

CUSTOMER-2:
Bartender! Bartender!

BARTENDER:
(*To Customer-1*) I'll be back, kiddo. Meantime you just chew on what I said.
(*To Customer-2*) What'll it be, partner?

CUSTOMER-2:
Give me a gun.

BARTENDER:
I've got Rusty Nails, Tequila Sunrises, Russian Mules and the Ultimate Marguerita, but I don't have a gun. Why don't you start off with this. (*The Bartender gives him a beer. Customer-2 drinks the beer the Bartender gives him.*)

CUSTOMER-2:
You want to kill me?

BARTENDER:
Was the drink that bad?

CUSTOMER-2:
No, but my life is. My second wife left me and took the three children.

BARTENDER:
Maybe you didn't appreciate them when you had them.

CUSTOMER-2:
So, Dr. Ruth, what's that supposed to mean?

BARTENDER:
Maybe you have some mending to do. Maybe you need to make some changes.

CUSTOMER-2:
　　Like what?

BARTENDER:
　　I've always tried to learn from my mistakes and move on. It's the little things I discovered were important in relationships: the flowers, the occasional card, finding a way, no matter how difficult it was at times, to say "I love you." (*Customer-3 comes in and sits down.*)
　　(*To Customer-2*) Excuse me. (*He goes to Customer-3 and pours him a beer.*) So, what's your story, Mac?

CUSTOMER-3:
　　Story?

BARTENDER:
　　Yeah. Everybody who comes in here has a story. As the song says: "Some drink to remember. Some drink to forget." Either way, they've all got a story.

CUSTOMER-3:
　　I'm a graduate of Santa Clara University. I was an Engineering major. I was valedictorian of my graduating class. I got a great job with Hewlett-Packard. During my first four years with them I received six promotions.

BARTENDER:
　　Well, Mac, it doesn't sound like you need to be here. Why are you here?

CUSTOMER-3:
　　Because I hate it.

BARTENDER:
　　Then why are you there?

CUSTOMER-3:
　　Because I make good money.

BARTENDER:

Are you happy?

CUSTOMER-3:

No, but with what I make I can go where I want, do what I want, and get what I want.

BARTENDER:

Then why are you in here, Mac? Figure that one out. (*Customer-3 is somewhat stunned.*)

CUSTOMER-3:

It's kinda deserted in here tonight.

BARTENDER:

It's always that way. (*The Bartender and three Customers freeze. Contestant-3 comes out and speaks.*)

CONTESTANT-3:

And when they gathered up the fragments, they filled twelve baskets.

SCENE TWO

ALL:

(*All the members of Scene One speak the opening and closing lines of Scene Two.*) Give them something to eat.

NARRATOR:

Good evening, and welcome to another edition of that heart-wrenching saga, "As the Garden Grows." Sponsored, in part, by Herbal Life: "Keeping the Mission Gardens Beautiful for over fifty years."

Today's episode finds Lorenzo Listener strolling through the Mission Gardens. In front of Media Services he bumps into Francine, a member of his Frosh Orientation Group. She looks exhausted, nervous and distraught.

LARRY:

Yo, Francine, mellow out. What are you walking in circles for?

FRANCINE:

Oh Larry, I don't know what to do. It's the end of the quarter and I'm in trouble! I have three papers due tomorrow that I haven't even found a topic for. I have four exams this week and I haven't read any of the material. I just know I'm going to get kicked out of Santa Clara.

NARRATOR:

Larry tries unsuccessfully to console Francine. But she rushes to the Kenna Computer Lab to fight for a Word Star disc she does not know how to use.

Continuing his leisurely stroll through the gardens, Larry spots Helen Heartthrob exiting St. Joseph's Hall. She sighs heavily to Larry.

HELEN:

Oh Larry, what on earth shall I ever do? My honey, Fred, the very air I breathe, the blood that runs through my veins, is leaving for the summer. Larry, you're a man. You know what ticks inside of them. Tell me the truth, even if it hurts. Will he be faithful to me? Will I ever see him again? What if he doesn't write? What if he doesn't call? What if he finds someone else? Whatever shall I do? Wherever shall I go?

NARRATOR:

Larry, who wants to escape this modern-day Scarlet O'Hara, tells Helen he is late for an appointment at the Faculty Club and sets a new U.S. and World Record for the hundred-meter dash.

In front of the Faculty Club Larry meets Steven, a senior, who is sporting a furrowed brow and hazardously drooping posture.

LARRY:

Yo, Steven, cheer up. It can't be all that bad!

STEVEN:

That's what you think! I haven't been accepted by any graduate schools. I've been interviewed by thirty companies and not one has called me back. I was a candidate for Valedictorian, the Nobili Medal and the St. Clare's Award. I didn't get any of them. And to top it all off, our commencement speaker is an unknown sociologist. When people ask me what I'm going to do after graduation, I tell them "starve." They think I'm kidding but I'm not!

NARRATOR:

Later, Larry sees Sue Zempathy in front of Nobili Hall. She seems upset.

LARRY:

Yo, Sue, what's your problem?

SUE:

Oh Larry, I'm concerned about my friends. I'm confused and don't know what to do. My best friend tried to commit suicide last week. I wonder if there was something I could have done to help prevent that. Yesterday five friends from my dorm were in a serious car accident. Today I found out that my roommate is pregnant. She doesn't want an abortion but she's not sure she wants a child either. Larry, why do these things happen? What am I supposed to think? How am I supposed to feel? What am I supposed to do?

NARRATOR:

Finally, in front of the theater, Larry runs into Danielle Dramatique. She is reciting a monologue from *Desire Under the Palms.* Larry interrupts her.

LARRY:

Yo, Danielle, how's by you?

DANIELLE:

Oh Larry, have you seen the review of the play? It was awful. That critic, Thelma Puce, has left no turn unstoned. With a review like that I'll never be considered for the parts I want. I auditioned for several summer stock companies in the area but they all turned me down. Maybe I should get out of acting and take up something more secure like being a stock market analyst.

NARRATOR:

Later by himself, Larry complains about his own fate.

LARRY:

Yo, Larry, why do you have to listen to all of these people? You got enough problems of your own. It's all just overwhelming. It's too much, way too much!

NARRATOR:

That evening at the 10 p.m. Mission liturgy, Larry sees Sue, Helen, Danielle, Steven and Francine. So he joins them. Each has come upset and confused. Each is searching for answers. Will Francine find what she needed to successfully complete the quarter? Will Helen's boyfriend dump her? Will Steven starve? Will Sue find the meaning of life? Will Danielle buy some summer stock? And what about Larry? None was prepared for what they were about to hear.

PRIEST:

At this time of the year, we are tired. I wouldn't be surprised if everyone in this church felt their life was out of control. A lot has been going on. Many here tonight feel confused, fragmented and alone, just like the characters in a soap opera. If faith tells us anything, it tells us we are not alone. The early Christians shared all things in common. That included what made them happy and sad: their experiences, their questions, their feelings, their hopes and dreams. Let's pray that God will help us do the same. (*Everyone in Scene Two freezes.*)

ALL:

And when they gathered up the fragments, they filled twelve baskets.

SCENE THREE

ALL:

(*The characters from Scenes One and Two now combine to do the lines at the beginning and end of Scene Three.*) Give them something to eat.

HOST:

Good evening, ladies and gentlemen, I'm Garth Ashbeck and I want to welcome you all to the newest game show in town, "You Give Them Something to Eat." Each week we challenge three contestants who have recently left university campuses to deal with contemporary human dilemmas. You the studio audience will judge which of them has learned something at school that can help them respond to our guests in need. So without further ado, let's meet our contestants. Contestant number one is Michelle Anselmo. Michelle, I see here you're from Venice, California. Tell us a little something about yourself.

CONTESTANT-1:

I'm a graduate of the University of San Francisco. I was philanthropy chairperson for my sorority. I majored in Finance and took a minor in Religious Studies. The person I most admire is Nancy Reagan . . . or Mother Teresa . . . er, Nancy Reagan and Mother Teresa.

HOST:

Contestant number two is Sean Murphy from South San Francisco. Tell us about yourself, Sean.

CONTESTANT-2:

I just graduated in Engineering from Stanford. I played on our NCAA National Champion Baseball, Tennis and Water Polo Teams. The people I most admire are Lee Iacocca, Lt. Oliver North and Attorney General Ed Meese.

HOST:

Contestant number three, I don't seem to have any information on you. Your name is?

CONTESTANT-3:

Cari.

HOST:

And what do you call home, Cari?

CONTESTANT-3:

The Julian Street Inn when they've got room, otherwise wherever I can find a little shelter and a place to lay my head.

HOST:

But what university campus have you recently been on?

CONTESTANT-3:

Well, I was recently asked to leave Santa Clara University's campus because I was a vagrant.

HOST:

I see. Well, that's not exactly the campus contact we were looking for, but welcome all the same. Contestants, you know the rules. Here's our first dilemma.

DILEMMA-1:

I'm a senior in college. I graduate this June. I think I would like to spend a year getting beyond the gates of Santa Clara. I was thinking about spending a year working for others in the Jesuit Volunteer Corps. Some of my friends advised me to get into Graduate School. My family think I should take one of the lucrative jobs I have been offered. I'm not sure what to do.

HOST:

O.K., panelists, what advice can you offer this young man?

CONTESTANT-1:

I wouldn't run the risk of losing those lucrative jobs. Think of all the good you could do with the money you'd make.

CONTESTANT-2:

Don't throw all that education away. If you get into grad school now you can make twice as much in two years with that graduate degree. Besides, they might stick you in some God-awful place in that Volunteer Corps you're thinking about. And then what would you do?

CONTESTANT-3:

Well, I'd say trust your instincts. I haven't had the chance to go to college, but I think I've learned a thing or two in my life. Some of the most important things I've learned weren't in the classroom. A lot of what you need to know in life comes from people and experiences not textbooks.

HOST:

And now let's move on to our second dilemma.

DILEMMA-2:

I'm a junior in college. At the beginning of the year I moved into an apartment off campus with four of my friends. Although I've tried to deny it and avoid it in a lot of ways, it's clear that one of my roommates has a serious drinking problem. I don't know what to do.

HOST:

O.K. panelists, what can you offer this person in need?

CONTESTANT-1:

I think it's irresponsible of your roommate. Drink and work are incompatible. My hunch is he will only drag you down with him. Get a new roommate.

CONTESTANT-2:

What's wrong with getting plastered now and then? You've got to blow off steam some way. Just cover the floor with newspaper in the event he gets sick.

CONTESTANT-3:

I know what drinking can do to you and those you love. Alcoholism is a disease. You don't need a college degree to know that. If you really care about your friend you need to confront the problem with him compassionately.

HOST:

Thank you, contestants, for your replies. Now let's move to our final dilemma.

DILEMMA-3:

I live in a dorm. One of my friends on my floor has been going through a lot of pain all year. Her mother died of cancer during the summer. I was afraid to ask her how her mother was when we returned in September. I didn't know what I could have said or done. So, I didn't say or do anything. I know this has hurt my friend very much. I feel a distance between us. Is there anything I can do now?

CONTESTANT-1:

Yewww! Death just sends chills up and down my back. It was a morbid subject then and it would be a morbid subject now. Don't dwell on the dismal. If your friend wants to be depressed, that's her business.

CONTESTANT-2:

Well, I've always found that when I was anxious or depressed that exercise helped. I would encourage you to get her out for a game of tennis or water polo. Don't dwell on the past, however. Focus on the future.

CONTESTANT-3:

Everybody's got a story, no matter how rich or poor, educated or uneducated they are. Many of us can't listen to and be present to the hard parts of other people's stories—like death—because they remind us of some of the painful parts of our own story. I don't ever think it's too late to say I made a mistake or I'm sorry. Perhaps if you can listen to your friend's pain and disappointment, she can understand the fear that silenced you and kept you away.

HOST:

Well, Contestants, our time is up. Now it's time for you, our audience, to vote. Which of our contestants gave these people in need something to eat. Was it Contestant number one, Contestant number two or Contestant number three? (*They all freeze.*)

ALL:

And when they gathered the fragments, they filled twelve baskets. (*Here all the characters in all three scenes stand and move to different parts of the sanctuary. They look at different people and slowly say the following line together.*)
You! Give them something to eat!

Finis

PROPS

1. Three bar stools.
2. One bar (a thin table would do nicely).
3. Glasses for the Bartender to be drying during the first scene as well as to use for pouring beer into them.
4. Two beer bottles with lager-colored liquid in them (ginger ale simulates beer nicely).
5. One backless bench that the characters in Scene Two can sit on when they gather in the Mission during the second scene.

PRODUCTION NOTES

This particular biblical dramatization was part of a liturgy that concluded a week at Santa Clara University where we were focusing on hunger in the world. If you do this in the United States, it might be extremely appropriate to enact this dramatization during the week prior to the celebration of Thanksgiving. To further your consciousness-raising about this problem and to find possible solutions, I encourage you to request materials from national organizations (e.g., *Oxfam America, Bread for the World, Catholic Relief Services,* etc.) or local community groups working with the hungry in your area.

While I listed props to create the impression of a bar for Scene One, glasses and bottles and tables can be quite cumbersome. Murphy's law states that "if something can go wrong, it generally will." Interpreted with regard to biblical dramatizations it suggests that if you use "breakable" props they very well may break during the course of their use. This can be a needless worry and distraction. The drying of glasses as well as the pouring and drinking of beer can all be mimed quite effectively and convincingly by your dramatists. All it takes is practice.

The second scene of this biblical dramatization should be done very broadly. It lends itself to the broad strokes and caricatures of a melodrama. Allow your players to have fun with this and explore the ways they can most effectively communicate what is happening among the characters.

There are numerous references in this biblical dramatization, as well as in other dramatizations in this volume, to Santa Clara University and parts of our campus and surrounding environs. These made a great deal of sense to our congregations/audiences but would evoke vacant stares and blank faces in yours. These local referents need to be changed/translated to local referents for your congregation and audience. One simple example would be the reference in Scene Three to Jesuit Universities. Since Santa Clara is a Jesuit University, our students are quite aware of other Jesuit institutions of higher learning in the state of California (i.e., University of San Francisco in San Francisco and Loyola Marymount in Los Angeles). It would probably be much more helpful for you to substitute names of colleges in your local area or state rather than use the ones we did. This is just one example of how to adapt these biblical dramatizations to your own people and needs.

REFLECTION QUESTIONS AND EXERCISES

1. Good dramas and good stories unfold through action. There are many actions in this biblical story about the feeding of the five thousand (Matt 14:13–21). What actions stand out for you or your reflection group? What strikes you about these actions? What are the attitudes and behaviors of the disciples in this biblical story? What are the actions and behaviors of the people who followed Jesus in this biblical story? What are the actions and behaviors of Jesus in this biblical story? How do you or your reflection group think you would have reacted if you had been in the position of the disciples? Would your attitudes or behaviors have been any different than theirs? Why or why not? Explain.

I would like you now to focus on four actions of this story that are found in verse nineteen. Those four actions are: (1) taking, (2) blessing, (3) breaking, and (4) sharing. How as human beings do we "take"? What do we take? Where do we take? When do we take? Why do we take? How, as human beings, do we "bless"? When do we bless? Why do we bless? How, as human beings, do we "break"? What do we break? When do we break? Why do we break? How, as human beings, do we "share"? What do we share? When do we share? Where do we share? Why do we share?

Dom Gregory Dix, in his book, *The Shape of the Liturgy* (London: Dacre Press, A & C Black, 1945, p. 48), described the fourfold action of eucharist (the Greek word *eucharistia* means "thanksgiving") as: taking, blessing, breaking and sharing. You will find these actions explicitly in any Christian eucharist. I invite you or your reflection group to imaginatively explore some of the other human experiences in which we take, bless, break and share. How many can you discover? In reflecting upon these questions and sharing your responses and faith in the process, aren't you taking, blessing, breaking and sharing? Doesn't that give this type of faith-sharing a eucharistic flavor?

2. I invite you or your reflection group to read the account of the feeding of the five thousand as it appears in Matthew

(Matt 14:13–21), Mark (Mk 6:30–44), and Luke (Lk 9:10–17). What differences do you or your reflection group find in the different accounts of this incident?

In Matthew's account of this biblical story, what good news do you or your reflection group find in it? Explain. What brokenness or sin do you or your reflection group find in this biblical story? To what kinds of change or conversion do you or your reflection group think this biblical story calls us?

Many of you who use this resource and these reflection questions will be culturally very similar to those of us who first created them. We come from the First World. Our brothers and sisters from the Third World (i.e., developing nations who experience great poverty and struggle as well as hope) can see and hear some very different things in these same biblical stories. I encourage you and your reflection group to read this biblical story from another perspective. A wonderful resource for this is Ernesto Cardenal's four-volume work entitled *The Gospel in Soletiname* (New York: Orbis Books, 1984). Read and reflect on "The Multiplication of the Loaves" (Vol. 2, p. 147) from the perspective of Cardenal's Base Community in Nicaragua. What good news do you think they hear in this biblical story? What brokenness or sin do you think they hear in this story? To what kinds of conversion does Cardenal's faith community think we are called? How do their reflections differ from yours or your group's? If they differ, why do you think they differ? I strongly encourage you to use this exercise wherever possible when reflection and sharing faith on gospel stories.

3. Albert Nolan, in his book, *Jesus Before Christianity* (New York: Orbis Books, 1978), offers some challenging insights into the meaning and significance of this biblical miracle story in chapter seven, entitled "The Kingdom and Money." Nolan contends that the best example of Jesus' attempts to educate the people to share what they had, was the miracle story about the feeding of the five thousand. If at all possible, I encourage you to read this chapter of Nolan's book. It is quite short. Do you or your reflection group agree or disagree with the above statement? Explain.

Nolan believes that this event has a deeper meaning and significance. He believes that the event itself was not a miracle of multiplication, but a remarkable example of sharing. What do you or your reflection group understand is the difference or distinction between "a miracle of multiplication" and "a remarkable example of sharing"? Do you or your reflection group agree or disagree with Nolan's interpretation of this biblical story? Explain. Do you find it difficult or easy to share with others? What do you find easy and satisfying about sharing? What do you find painful or difficult about sharing? Does our culture and society encourage or discourage sharing today? How do culture and society do this? Does the church encourage or discourage sharing today? How does the church do this?

Nolan believes that "the real 'miracle' was that so many people should suddenly cease to be possessive about their food and begin to share, only to discover that there was more than enough to go around. . . . Things do tend to 'multiply' when you share them" (p. 52). Do you or your reflection group agree or disagree with his interpretation of these events? Explain.

Nolan goes on to connect this biblical miracle story with the attitudes and behaviors of the early Christian community described in the Acts of the Apostles. He says: "This then is what selling one's possessions means; giving up the surplus and treating nothing as your own. The result will always be that 'none of their members was ever in want' (Acts 4:34)." What do you or your reflection group think about such attitudes and behaviors? What would happen if Christian communities had similar attitudes and behaviors today? Would people think they were crazy? Why or why not? Explain. Nolan concludes his chapter with an extremely challenging statement: "It follows that any society that is so structured that some suffer because of their poverty, and others have more than they need, is part of the kingdom of Satan." What do you or your reflection group think Nolan means by this statement? Do you or your reflection group agree or disagree with Nolan's evaluation? Explain.

4. In the first scene of the biblical dramatization, the Bartender invites people to share their stories. I invite you and your

reflection group to engage in some story telling and story listening. This is one of the ways we discover who we are and communicate that to others. This is also one of the ways we discover who others are and how they communicate that to us. While we will be using words to tell our stories, you can have stories told without words. Look at people's faces on a crowded bus or subway. Pay attention to the way people walk or carry themselves as they walk along the street. Buried deep in these bodily expressions and actions are stories.

Where do you come from? Describe the place (city/state/country) in which you were born. Describe your parents and family. Describe your brothers and sisters, if you have any. What strengths of your parents or family do you see in yourself? What weaknesses or deficiencies of your parents or family do you see in yourself?

Who are some of the friends that you like? What do you like most about them? Who are some of the people (living or dead) that you most admire? What qualities or characteristics do you admire in them?

If you could only describe yourself in four words (they don't have to be connected to make a phrase or sentence), what four words would you choose, at this time, to describe yourself to others? Explain why you would choose each of these words as descriptive of yourself.

5. Do you ever feel as if you are living your life like a character in a soap opera? Can you identify with the concerns of any of the characters in Scene Two of this biblical dramatization? Why or why not? Explain. What do you or your reflection group think about the priest's advice to those attending mass? Do you think his advice is helpful? Why or why not? Explain. Would you consider the priest's words "truthful" or "sound advice"? Why or why not? Explain.

In the third chapter of the first Book of Kings (1 Kgs 3:4–15), there is a story about God appearing to Solomon in a dream. God tells Solomon to ask for whatever he wants and God will give it to him. Solomon asks for "an understanding heart." What do you or your reflection group think Solomon means by "an understanding heart"? How might "an understanding heart" help you deal with experiences of confusion or conflict in your life?

Meister Eckhart, a fourteenth-century German Dominican mystic, described "wisdom" as: "the ability to do the next thing you have to do; do it with your whole heart; and take delight in doing it." Do any of the characters in Scene Two exhibit this wisdom in their attitudes or behavior? Why or why not? Explain. Do you exhibit this type of wisdom in your attitude or behavior? Why or why not? Explain. If not, would you like to exhibit this kind of wisdom in your attitude and behavior? Why or why not? Explain. What would you have to change in your life in order to do this?

6. In the biblical dramatization, Dilemma-1 talks about J.V.C. (The Jesuit Volunteer Corps). This is a program open to those who have graduated from university. Participants volunteer a year of their life to explore the four components of J.V.C. life: (1) a simple life-style, (2) living in community (with other volunteers), (3) growing in one's spirituality (i.e., your relationship with God), and (4) exploring the connections between faith and the ways it is expressed in working for justice in our society. What do you or your reflection group think might be the value of living "a simple life-style"? What would be some of the challenges that living simply would present you with? What do you or your reflection group think might be the value of "living in community"? What do you think might be some of the challenges of living together in community? What do you or your reflection group think might be the value of growing and developing your "spirituality"? What do you think might be some of the challenges of growing in your relationship with God? What do you or your reflection group think might be the value of "exploring the connections between faith and justice"? What do you think might be some of the challenges of exploring such connections?

The Jesuit Volunteer Corps has a motto: "Join the J.V.C. and be ruined for life." What do you or your reflection group think that they mean by this? Find out if there are any J.V.C. volunteers or communities near you. Invite some of the members to come and share with you what their experiences have been during a year of volunteer service in the J.V.C. What questions surface for

you or your reflection group about community service like the
J.V.C.?

Substance abuse programs are often run by local hospitals.
Invite a representative from one of these substance abuse programs to come and share with your group about addiction and
how you treat it.

There are a variety of grief counseling services available to
people. Oftentimes we are unaware of this help and assistance.
As human beings we are constantly exposed to experiences of
life and death. Invite someone who works in grief counseling to
come and share with you and your reflection group about how
we can learn to deal with experiences of death in our own life
and how we can be humanly supportive of those around us who
have experienced a death in their life.

7. Have you ever found yourself in a situation similar to
those described by Dilemma-1, Dilemma-2 or Dilemma-3? Did
you do anything about it? Why or why not? Explain.

What do you or your reflection group think about the advice
given to Dilemma-1 by the contestants in Scene Three? What
advice would you or your reflection group offer to Dilemma-1?

What do you or your reflection group think about the advice
given to Dilemma-2 by the contestants in Scene Three? What
advice would you or your reflection group offer to Dilemma-2?

What do you or your reflection group think about the advice
given to Dilemma-3 by the contestants in Scene Three? What
advice would you or your reflection group offer to Dilemma-3?

Which of the contestants gave Dilemma-1 something to eat?
Explain. Which of the contestants gave Dilemma-2 something to
eat? Explain. Which of the contestants gave Dilemma-3 something to eat? Explain. Who are the people in your life who have
given you something to eat when you were most in need of it?
How did they do this for you? How do you or your reflection
group think that you can give other people in your life something
to eat? Explain.

8. Tissa Balisuriya, in his book, *Jesus, The Eucharist and
Human Liberation* (New York: Orbis Books, 1979), makes a very
challenging statement. He says that "unless there is this twofold

dimension of personal love and societal action, eucharist runs the risk of becoming a sacrilege" (p. 22). If possible, read Balisuriya's short chapter in which he makes this statement (pp. 16–22). How would you or your reflection group define a sacrilege? What behaviors might be sacrilegious? What attitudes might be behind such behavior? What do you or your reflection group think Balisuriya means by saying that our experience of eucharist must have a dimension of "personal love"? Explain.

What do you or your reflection group think Balisuriya means by saying that our experience of eucharist must have a dimension of "societal action"? Explain. What do you or your reflection group think is the relationship between "personal love" and "societal action" that Balisuriya is talking about? Explain. Do you agree or disagree with Balisuriya's statement? Explain.

7. A Sabbath Cure

(Luke 13:10-17)

Now he was teaching in one of the synagogues on the sabbath. And there was a woman who had had a spirit of infirmity for eighteen years; she was bent over and could not fully straighten herself. And when Jesus saw her, he called her and said to her, "Woman, you are freed from your infirmity." And he laid his hands upon her, and immediately she was made straight, and she praised God. But the ruler of the synagogue, indignant because Jesus had healed on the sabbath, said to the people, "There are six days on which work ought to be done;

come on those days and be healed, and not on the sabbath day." Then the Lord answered him, "You hypocrites!
Does not each of you on the sabbath untie his ox or his
ass from the manger, and lead it away to water it? And
ought not this woman, a daughter of Abraham whom
Satan bound for eighteen years, be loosed from this bond
on the sabbath day?" As he said this, all his adversaries
were put to shame; and all the people rejoiced at all the
glorious things that were done by him.

The Truth Will Set You Free

CAST

Outer	Student-1
Inner	Student-2
Parent	Student-3
School	David
Boyfriend	Brian
Religion	Duck-1
Duck-2	Duck-3
Donald	Daisy
Person-1	Person-2
Person-3	Person-4
Person-5	Person-6
Person-7	

SCENE ONE

[*Two characters, one called "Inner" and the other called "Outer" represent two parts of the same person. The "Outer" is the part of us that everyone sees. The "Inner" is what that character is really thinking. These two parts of one whole will run through each of the three scenes. The "Inner" will also become the focal character in each of the three scenes.*]

OUTER:

I hate spring quarter! I hate school! I hate all my classes! I especially hate Biblical Drama Class! Why do we have to keep a dumb journal anyway? I hate journals!

INNER:

Well, Krista, you've procrastinated long enough. Whether you like it or not, you have to make an entry in your journal. So you might as well get off your duff and start thinking and writing.

OUTER:

May 18th. Today in Biblical Drama Class. . . . (*Outer thinks for a moment and then smiles.*)

. . . we all were bitten by diseased rats and contracted the dreaded bubonic plague. Fifty-six of Santa Clara's finest students shall all die within the next two weeks. What a loss! What a tragedy! And this senseless catastrophe was all caused by BIBLICAL DRAMA!

INNER:

Ahem! After your brief comic break, are you ready to get to work, Krista?

OUTER:

May 18th. Today in Biblical Drama Class we worked with the story from Luke's gospel of Jesus curing the woman who had been bent over with a spirit of infirmity for eighteen years. I suppose the most interesting thing that the teacher said about this story was that there were three main characters in it: a crippled person, a righteous person, and a Christ. Fr. Moynahan only confused me when he said that we have all three characters inside of us. Sounds like something a Jesuit would say. Kind of confusing, if you ask me.

INNER:

Confusing or not, ask the reflection questions he told you to explore.

OUTER:

Who or what in us is crippled and in need of healing? What a crazy question! I'm not stooped over like that woman was. I wonder how I'm supposed to figure out the experiences and things that cripple me or tie me in knots?

INNER:

>Not on the outside, Krista, but what about the inside? (*Outer freezes while Inner moves over to the center stage and is surrounded by four different people who have red and white twine. As each person speaks to Inner they bind her in some way.*)

PARENT:

>Krista, your father and I are pretty disappointed. Your sister has been getting in all sorts of trouble. She's become the class clown.

INNER:

>But Mom, I'm three thousand miles away. How is this all my fault?

PARENT:

>If you had set a better example, Krista, we think your sister would never have gotten into all this trouble.

SCHOOL:

>It's the end of your senior year, Krista, and you still have not declared a major.

INNER:

>But I'm just not sure.

SCHOOL:

>Time is money, Krista. How much are you willing to spend before you make up your mind?

BOYFRIEND:

>You can't keep me dangling like this, Krista. Is there something between us or not?

INNER:

>I like you Chris. I like you a lot. Yes, I want a relationship with you but as a friend, not a lover.

BOYFRIEND:

Krista, that's about as appealing as a free bid to a boat dance on the Titanic!

RELIGION:

Your principles are about as strong as freshly poured jello. You say your faith is important to you but you wouldn't be caught dead in a church. You say you believe in honesty but your relationships feed on lies. You say you want to love people in actions and not just words but you never seem to have time to take advantage of any volunteer opportunities. You, Krista, are a walking contradiction!

INNER:

I want to believe. I want to be truthful. I want to help. But it's not always as simple as that. (*The four people sit down and Inner moves back toward Outer.*)

SCENE TWO

OUTER:

Well, no use overdoing it! So, alright, maybe we are bound or crippled in a few ways. But this second question is just not relevant. How are we righteous? What part of us is hypocritical?

INNER:

Don't dismiss it too quickly, Krista. Remember last Thursday when the newspaper came out and you were in class? Remember all the events of that day? (*Outer takes a thoughtful pose and freezes. Inner moves into the classroom scene on the center stage.*)

STUDENT-1:

So who does he think he is, Charles Atlas?

STUDENT-2:
I think he's kind of stuck on himself.

STUDENT-3:
I've turned down two invitations to the senior ball waiting for him to call.

STUDENT-1:
Well, don't be too disappointed if he flakes out on you.

STUDENT-3:
What do you mean?

STUDENT-2:
He may have saved you from a long, boring evening.

STUDENT-1:
His conversation is "how you say" limited. If you're not talking about something he's done or done more often or better than you, he doesn't have much to say.

STUDENT-2:
Yeah, Dave's really a pathological liar. You can't believe a word he says. (*David comes into the class area. The Students gesture and make signs to one another to switch the conversation.*)

DAVID:
Hey, what's up? This looks like a Security Council meeting.

INNER:
We were just talking about you. (*The three Students look at Inner with angry and shocked looks of betrayal.*)

STUDENT-3:
Yeah, we were wondering how you did on Dr. Bogucki's mid-term.

DAVID:

> Absolutely the pits! I studied five days for that test. The questions were vague. He tested us on material we never covered in class.

STUDENT-1:

> He shouldn't be teaching sociology at this school.

STUDENT-2:

> No, he should open his own Academy of Cruel and Unusual Punishment.

STUDENT-3:

> Subjecting us to someone like him must violate some constitutional right we have.

INNER:

> Oh, oh. Here comes Dr. Frankenstein himself!

DAVID:

> I'd be willing to bet that Dr. Dorko will give us a pop quiz!

BRIAN:

> Alright class, I'd like to spend a little time talking about the "Color of Our Skin" series which recently focused our attention on various forms of racism and prejudice. What exactly are we talking about when we speak of "prejudice" in any form? (*David raises his hand.*)
> Marcy.

STUDENT-3:

> It literally means to judge something or someone before we actually experience them.

BRIAN:

> And why do you think this type of "pre-judging" occurs? (*David raises his hand.*)
> Brennan.

STUDENT-1:

I think we fear what we don't know. Prejudice is a very dangerous and unhealthy "defense mechanism."

BRIAN:

What would be some of our cultural and ethnic stereotypes that would be examples of racist thinking? (*David raises his hand again.*)

Cari.

STUDENT-2:

All blacks are good atheletes but are not very intelligent. All Asians are bright and play chess. All Hispanics belong to gangs, come from barrios and drive "Chebbies with Dingle Balls." All Hawaiians eat poi and know how to hula.

BRIAN:

And what would be another form of prejudice we might find on this campus besides racism? (*David raises his hand again and is obviously frustrated.*)

Ahhhhh. . . .

DAVID:

(*David blurts out.*) Sexism. Discriminating against a person because of their gender or sex!

BRIAN:

That's right, David, but please don't speak unless you are called upon.

DAVID:

Well, I think hell would freeze over before you called on a male in this class.

BRIAN:

Dave, if you have a complaint, please see me in my office. I see our time is just about up. We will continue exploring prejudice and sexism next class. (*Brian leaves.*)

DAVID:
That's it! We have got to put an end to this.

STUDENT-3:
But how?

STUDENT-2:
Yeah. What can we do?

DAVID:
We've at least got the class evaluations. We've got to put how rotten he really is on those evaluations.

STUDENT-1:
Dave, it's no use. They won't even read our evaluations.

STUDENT-3:
And even if they do, it won't change anything! (*The three Students get up and leave. Inner stays there as Dave is given a paper.*)

INNER:
Cheer up, Dave. Did you get a copy of this week's paper?

DAVID:
No. (*Inner hands him one and he opens it and begins to read.*)
A special feature on "Women in Society." Just what I needed to "make my day!" A turn of the tide . . . sounds like they're war correspondents. Many college students suffer from anorexia and bulimia . . . geees, great way to ruin a guy's appetite. Feminists attempt to liberate both sexes . . . liberation, smibberation! Campus Ministry Director reflects on women in the Church. . . . That's part of the problem. What business has this University got making a woman Director of Campus Ministry? Before you know it, they're going to want a woman to be a University Vice President. Workshop deals with women's silence . . . not enough of it, if you ask me. If women are so great, I'd like to see them make babies without us!

INNER:

With some higher developed forms of life they actually do. (*David freezes with puzzled look and Inner moves back to Outer.*)

SCENE THREE

OUTER:

Alright, so we're human, at times, and guilty of some occasional inconsistency. So that's a capital offense?

INNER:

And how are you going to tackle that last question, Krista?

OUTER:

This one is really preposterous! How am I like Christ? What on earth does he mean?

INNER:

In what ways are you called to be a healing presence or part of the healing process for others? (*Outer begins to think.*)

And the healing may not always mean being kinder and gentler. Sometimes healing begins with a shock: an ending of an experience we like, the death of a loved one, unwanted change and transition in a relationship, facing the truth about ourselves we have denied or avoided for too long a time. But the shock is what often brings about the development of unrealized potential in us. The same thing happens in the animal world. (*They both freeze as the Ducks come alive on center stage. The three baby ducks are gradually joined by Donald and Daisy.*)

DUCK-1:

Quack. Quack. Here come Mom and Dad.

DUCK-2:

Quack. Quack. Their eyesight isn't what it used to be. We could be looking at a head-on collision.

DUCK-3:

Quack. Quack. So you know what that means. Everybody DUCK!!! Quack! Quack! (*The three Ducks quack in delight. Donald and Daisy join them in their nest.*)

DONALD:

O.K. kids, stifle your quacks.

DAISY:

Quiet down, children, and listen to your father.

DONALD:

Dear, they look awfully hungry. Maybe we should have some cheese and quackers before I begin. (*They all quack.*)

DAISY:

Now Donald, I want you to take the duck by the bill and get on with it.

DONALD:

Oh alright! Children, there comes a time in every duck's life when he . . .

DAISY:

Or she . . .

DONALD:

Thank you dear . . . or she must leave the nest.

DUCK-1:

But we like it in here!

DUCK-2:

It's warm. It's secure! It's home!

DUCK-3:

Go ahead. Throw us out into the damp and cold. We should have known it was too good to last . . . that one day we would grow up to be . . .

DUCKS:

ORPHANED DUCKS! (*All the small Ducks begin quacking and crying.*)

DUCK-1:

But we don't want to leave.

DAISY:

If you don't go, you'll never grow.

DUCK-2:

But there's water all around us. We'll drown!

DONALD:

No you won't. Your mother and I felt the same way. We didn't know, as you don't know, that we're all natural swimmers.

DUCK-3:

We won't sink?

DAISY:

No dear. You've got oil in your feathers. You can't sink.

DONALD:

It's duckatomically impossible. Alright now. No more dilly-dallying . . . off you go. (*Donald and Daisy start pushing the little ducks out of the nest as they quack up a storm. When they all get out, Donald and Daisy look proud and the Ducks look surprised as they swim to different parts of the congregation. They freeze.*)

INNER:

Just think of the shocks, the challenges, the growth of the past four years. (*Inner goes to center stage and surrounded by seven people, all of whom have pieces of red and white yarn hanging from their arms and necks, etc. They have obviously been cut.*)

PERSON-1:

Do you remember when you came into Campus Ministry that first week you came to Santa Clara? You hadn't been here forty-eight hours and yet you were sure everyone on your floor hated you and you had nothing in common with anyone at this school. You were homesick. You were lonesome. You were miserable and wanted to go home. I told you then the little story about Buddha, how it was said that he never attained enlightenment until he got beyond his parents' gates. You accepted the advice reluctantly. A year later you spoke those same words convincingly to your homesick roommate. Some things just take time.

PERSON-2:

Even though I told you to mind your own business, you were a friend to me by speaking the truth when I was afraid to hear it. When everyone else was amused by or ignored the dangerous amounts of alcohol I consumed, week after week, you loved me enough to tell me I had a problem. It took some time before I could hear what you were really saying, but you stuck with me and showed me how to find the help I needed.

PERSON-3:

I think you were as frightened of my cancer as I was. You didn't know what to say. Who does? But it didn't matter. You didn't run away from the awkwardness and fear. You were there. You held my hand. You helped me face my fear of dying. You took the time to teach me how to let go, how to trust.

PERSON-4:

When everyone else on the floor found it easier to ignore me or pretend I wasn't there, you always seemed to notice. I'll never forget your taking the time and making the effort to include me. And when a group of us did that floor event on racism, you knew it was important to me. You took the time to convince some others that it was a problem that concerned us all whether we were aware of it or not.

PERSON-5:

When I didn't want to deal with approaching graduation, when I didn't want to deal with that jumble of feelings that endings stir within me, when I simply wanted to postpone "goodbyes," you told me to take the time to remember and feel and express the sadness and joy and hundred other things I was feeling inside. You took the time to do that yourself and so challenged me to do the same.

PERSON-6:

Isn't it funny how giving doesn't diminish you? Life is full of paradoxes. Because you took time in your already busy schedule to help me, the experience called good and gifts out of you that you never knew existed. You helped me and taught me through your volunteer work how important it is to put the hungers, the hurts and needs of others before my own.

PERSON-7:

You do not know my face. You do not know my name. I am, as yet, unknown to you. My name is mystery, possibility, the future. All you have to do is trust me enough to allow me to unfold, one day at a time. Meet me, embrace me, enjoy me, discover who you really are and what you are becoming. Experience the wisdom and the wonder of learning to do the next thing you have to do, learning to do it with all your heart, and learning to take delight in doing it. (*Here the Outer comes and joins the Inner.*)

OUTER:

For three dumb questions, I sure have written an awful lot.

INNER:

Dumb questions or haunting questions? Questions you can never completely answer.

OUTER:

Dear Journal, that's it for this time. I'll have to do this again, spend some time reflecting on some good old dumb . . .

(*Inner looks at Outer.*) . . . haunting questions, real soon. (*All freeze.*)

Finis

PROPS

1. Twelve long pieces of red and white yarn which will be worn by four characters (Parent, School, Boyfriend and Religion) in Scene One.
2. Twenty-one pieces of red and white yarn worn by seven characters in Scene Three.
3. Five plastic or rubber duck bills. These are worn over the nose and held in place by a piece of elastic attached to them.
4. One journal.
5. One writing instrument (e.g., a pencil or a pen).

PRODUCTION NOTES

This biblical dramatization was part of a liturgy celebrated during a winter quarter at Santa Clara University. A group of students had organized a wonderfully educational and timely series on prejudice and discrimination entitled "The Color of Our Skin." That series took place during the same winter quarter. The Biblical Explorers once again attempted to allow contemporary events and experiences to shed new light on the possible meanings of scripture.

I am relatively sure that everyone's first reaction to the questions: "Are you prejudiced in any way?" "Do you discriminate unfairly in your attitudes and behaviors?" would be an emphatic and dramatic "No!" Upon careful examination, however, we may be surprised and shocked at some of the unconscious ways we can communicate prejudice and discrimination in our attitudes and behaviors.

In Roman Catholic worship, as in most Christian worship, there is a place for acknowledging our sinfulness and asking for God's forgiveness. In the *confiteor* we ask God's forgiveness for the ways we have sinned through our own fault, in our thoughts and in our words, in what we have done and what we have failed to do. How often are the jokes we tell or stories we repeat, that portray a race, a sex or any group of people in a foolish light, unconscious forms of discrimination? What if we are not the one who tells the insulting joke about blacks, Jews, women, gays, the Polish, the Irish or Italians, but the one who even uncomfortably laughs and through our laughter assents to the prolongation of ultimately damaging stereotypes? With prejudice and discrimination there are sins of commission and sins of omission (i.e., "in what I have done and what I have failed to do").

Scene Two has the character David reading a copy of the school newspaper toward the end of the scene. The issues he articulates were ones deeply affecting our campus at the time. They were areas of concern for us. I encourage you to adapt these issues and this biblical dramatization so that you can more appropriately address and challenge areas where your class or community need to grow in awareness of conscious and unconscious forms of prejudice and discrimination.

You will note that the biblical dramatization requires the use of red and white pieces of yarn. If ribbon will show up better than yarn, use that for the material worn around characters' arms and necks. The only significance of the colors "red" and "white" was that those happen to be Santa Clara University's school colors. Use whatever material and colors would best serve your production needs and purposes.

REFLECTION QUESTIONS AND EXERCISES

1. This biblical story about the healing of the crippled woman on the sabbath (Lk 13:10–17), is found only in the gospel of Luke. What Jesus does for this woman is the fulfillment of his commission of releasing captives from the bonds of evil. ("The Gospel According to Luke" commentary by Robert J. Karris, O.F.M. in the *New Jerome Biblical Commentary*.)

Jesus had spoken earlier in Luke's gospel about the nature and direction of his ministry when he quoted the prophet Isaiah

(Lk 4:18–19). Since all Christians are disciples of Christ and attempt to follow in the footsteps of the Teacher, I invite you or your reflection group to consider the following questions in light of Jesus' envisioned ministry and this miracle story.

How has the spirit of the Lord been given to you? How has God anointed you? For what has God anointed you?

What does it mean to you or your reflection group to be sent? How are we sent? What are we sent to say or do? What are some of the ways that Jesus brought good news to the poor? Who are the poor in our society and culture? Who are the poor outside our society and culture? How do we bring good news to the poor? What shapes and expressions will that good news take? Explain.

What do you or your reflection group think it means to proclaim liberty to captives in our day? Who are captives in our culture and society? Who are captives outside our culture and society? What would liberty mean for these different captives? How do we proclaim liberty to them? How do our actions proclaim louder and more powerfully than our words? What shapes and expressions will that liberty take? Explain.

What do you or your reflection group think it means to bring sight to the blind? Who are the blind in our culture and society? Who are the blind outside our culture and society? What can culture and society blind us to? What would sight consist in for those who are blind? What would sight mean for those who are blind? How do we bring sight to the blind? What shapes and expressions will this sight take? Explain.

What do you or your reflection group think it means to set the downtrodden free. Who are the downtrodden in our culture and society? Who are the downtrodden outside of our culture and society? What are the things that contribute to these people being downtrodden? What would freedom consist in for the downtrodden? How do we bring freedom to the downtrodden? What shapes and expressions will this freedom take? Explain.

What do you or your reflection group think it means to proclaim a year of favor from the Lord? What would it mean to people in our culture and society? What would it mean to people outside our culture and society? How would we proclaim this year of favor from the Lord? What shapes and expressions would this proclamation take? Explain.

2. A colleague of mine, and masterful storyteller, Margie Brown, once came and worked with a preaching class that I was teaching. I had asked her to share with the students some creative ways that they might be able to explore biblical stories and possibly uncover as yet undiscovered meaning in those stories. I invite you or your reflection group to experience this biblical miracle story through the creative dramatic process that Margie Brown shared with those preaching students.

The first thing that you do is familiarize yourself with the characters, the dialogue and the actions of the story. An easy way to do this is by having different members of your reflection group slowly read the biblical story out loud to the entire group.

Now invite each member of your reflection group to clear away a space in the room where they can operate. You will be using some mime in this process (i.e., you will be engaged in physical action without speaking). When everyone has their own piece of "cleared space" in the room, you might want to put on some gentle instrumental music. You can, however, do this exercise in silence. If people are somewhat self-conscious about doing physical movement in the same space with others, have them face the wall or keep their eyes closed during the exercise. The more focused the individual becomes on the actions of the exercise, the less aware they will be of the presence of other people in the room. If everyone is concentrating on the exercise, you will have no time to be observing the movement of others.

I will be asking you or your reflection group to go into this biblical story five times. The first time, I want you to go through this biblical story and physically become every noun (i.e., person, object, place, etc.) you can remember from this story. Don't hurry. Take your time. If a noun suggests itself that you don't remember being in the biblical story, embody it anyway. Do not censor. It is sometimes quite remarkable what will float up from the subconscious in this exercise. You may not understand its importance, at the time, but later it may become clear why this noun suggested itself for your physicalization. After you have become all of the nouns in this biblical story, come back to a place of rest and relaxation.

The second time, I want you to go through the biblical story and become every verb or action in this story. Physically act out every action that you can think of that takes place in this biblical story. When you have exhausted all the verbs or actions that you can think of, come back to a place of rest and relaxation.

The third time you go into this story, I want you to become all of the interactions between characters in this story. Physically act out every interaction between characters that takes place in this biblical story. Remember that there is no "right" or "wrong" way to physicalize these interactions, only the ways they imaginatively suggest themselves to you. When you have exhausted all of the interactions between characters, come back to a place of rest and relaxation.

The fourth time you go into this story, I want you to understand that this story has a question just for you. Listen for that question. When you hear it, and you may have to wait some time before you can hear it, give physical shape to that question (i.e., act it out). When you have done this, come back to a place of rest and relaxation.

The fifth and final time you go into this story, I want you to understand that this story has a gift or treasure just for you. Listen to what that gift or treasure is. When you hear it, and you may have to wait patiently for some time before you can hear it, give physical shape to that gift or treasure (i.e., act it out). When you have done this, come back to a place of rest and relaxation. Offer a silent prayer of thanks for the imaginative ways God has been with you through this exercise.

I encourage you to conclude this exercise by inviting the participants to share what they experienced as they moved through the biblical story in this imaginative way. What did you experience? What did you learn about this story that you didn't realize before?

3. I would like to invite you or your reflection group to explore this biblical story through the use of a creative dramatic technique called *tableaux vivant*. I describe and demonstrate this and other creative dramatic tools for exploring the riches of biblical material in a video program and written guide produced by Tabor Publishing Company in Allen, Texas. *Tableaux vivant* are like photographs with living people in them. The characters

in the pictures are still but express the action and feeling of the story through their physical and facial expressions.

I invite your reflection group to read this miracle story together. When you are finished, someone act as a recorder and invite everyone to brainstorm on the "pictures" they see in this biblical story. Your ultimate goal is to tell this biblical story through five or six (no more than six) pictures. Don't censor or reject any suggestions. Just get them all out on the table.

Now go through all the possible pictures you have and decide what five or six pictures will best visually communicate this story for your group. You may have to combine a couple of suggested pictures into one.

Next, have people in your reflection group assume the roles of the different biblical characters in this story. Begin practicing the re-creation of the different pictures you have decided on. Have someone step out from the pictures and make comments on what is or isn't being communicated through the different body positions and facial expressions in the particular picture.

When you have practiced the pictures, go back and run through them sequentially. You may be fortunate enough to do this in front of another group. After you have gone through this process, consider the following reflection questions.

(a) What pictures did you include in your *tableau vivant*? What did you learn about your understanding of this biblical story from the pictures you chose to do?

(b) What pictures did you exclude from your *tableau vivant*? What did you learn about your understanding of this biblical story from the pictures you chose to leave out?

(c) What, if anything, did you learn about the meaning of this biblical story through the experience of the *tableaux vivant* process? Explain.

(d) Did your initial understanding of this biblical story change at all as a result of exploring it with *tableaux vivant*? Why or why not? Explain.

(e) What understanding of Christ (christology) is communicated through the pictures you chose? In your pictures, how does Jesus heal? In your pictures, how does Jesus react to the woman who is crippled? In your pictures, how does Jesus react to the objections of the Temple Official?

4. In many of the miracle stories you will find three main characters: (a) someone in need of healing, (b) a righteous person, and (c) Christ. I invite you or your reflection group to consider these three characters as symbolic of different aspects of yourself. In light of this, consider the following questions. I invite you to spend some time reflecting on these questions and writing your responses in your journal. You may choose to share some of your reflections with your group after an appropriate period of time has been allowed for the reflecting and writing.

What does the crippled person symbolize in you? What part of you is crippled and in need of healing? What parts of yourself are incomplete and cry out for wholeness and healing?

What does the righteous person symbolize in you? What part of you hides comfortably behind the security and observance of the law? What parts of yourself are judgmental of the words and actions of others?

What does the Christ character symbolize in you? What parts of yourself are Christlike? What aspects of your attitudes and behaviors need healing for those around you?

5. In this exercise I ask you to go into this story in four imaginative ways. First of all, you are a newspaper reporter who witnesses all of the events of this biblical story as they unfold. Write a brief newspaper article describing the events that took place and people's reactions as you observed them and interviewed the characters afterwards. What did the woman who had been crippled say to you? What did the Temple Official have to say to you? What did Jesus have to say to you?

Now become the woman who was crippled. Experience the events of this story from inside her person. Later that evening, after being miraculously cured by this Jesus, you make an entry in your diary in which you try to capture some of the marvelous events that took place as well as your reactions to them. What do you write?

Now become the Temple Official. Experience the events of this story from inside his character. Later that evening, after this disturbing encounter with Jesus and the woman who had been crippled, you sit down and write a letter to your religious superior in which you describe the events and your reactions to them. What do you write?

Finally become Jesus. Experience the events of this story from inside of his character. Later that evening, after the disciples have gone to sleep, you bring the events of this day and your reactions to them to prayer. You either make a journal entry or compose a prayer that incorporates the people, the actions and your responses to all that happened in the Temple this day. What do you write or pray?

What do you or your reflection group learn about this biblical story and yourself from this exercise? Explain.

6. How would you or your reflection group define prejudice? Would you agree or disagree with the definition given in Scene Two that prejudice literally means to judge something before we actually experience it? Why or why not? Explain.

Oftentimes we may be unaware of our prejudices. Have you ever discovered that you judged a person, before you had a chance to genuinely know them, on the basis of:

(a) the color of their skin?

(b) their ethnic origins?

(c) their nationality?

(d) their gender (a man or a woman)?

(e) their religion (e.g., Christian, Buddhist, Hindu, Moslem, etc.)?

(f) their denomination (e.g., Roman Catholic, Lutheran, Episcopalian, Presbyterian, Methodist, Baptist, etc.)?

(g) their age?

(h) their physical condition (i.e., able-bodied or differently-abled)?

What shapes or expressions did your prejudice or discrimination take? How did you become aware of these prejudicial and discriminatory attitudes and behaviors?

Have you or your reflection group ever experienced prejudice or discriminatory behavior from others because of:

(a) the color of your skin?

(b) your ethnic background?

(c) your nationality?
(d) your gender?
(e) your religion?
(f) your denomination?
(g) your age?
(h) your physical condition?
What shapes and expression did this prejudice or discrimination take? Explain. What were your reactions to this prejudice and discrimination?

7. What do you or your reflection group think a stereotype is? What would be some examples of cultural, ethnic or gender stereotypes that you or your reflection group can identify? How do these stereotypes represent sexist or racist thinking?

The second scene of the biblical dramatization focuses on prejudice. What do you or your reflection group think are some of the more obvious forms of prejudice? Please come up with as many examples as possible. Write them on a chalk board or on a large piece of poster board. What do you or your reflection group think are some of the less obvious and more subtle forms of prejudice? Please come up with as many examples as possible. Write them on a chalk board or large piece of poster board.

If prejudice consists of fear of what we do not know or intense dislike of that which is different than us, how do you or your reflection group think we can address the ignorance and dislikes that have found expression in the obvious and subtle forms of prejudice you have listed? Focus first on one. When you have worked your way through that prejudice you may have some clues on how to deal with others.

8. In the "Reflection Questions and Exercises" that appeared after the biblical dramatization "Bartimaeus," I invited you to create a cinquain on "discipleship." I invite you now to use this creative technique with this biblical story about the healing of the woman who was crippled. Remember that a cinquain is a five-line piece of poetry. The first line consists of the word that is the subject or title of the poetic reflection. The second line consists of two descriptive adjectives that deal with your subject. The third line consists of three participles (i.e., action words,

verbs ending in "ing") that capture active dimensions of your first-line subject. The fourth line consists of a four word descriptive phrase that summarizes your subject. The fifth line consists in a one word restatement of your first line subject. The final line/word usually brings out some nuanced dimension of the first line/word and is an emphatic or gentle restatement of it.

I invite you or your reflection group to create a cinquain that captures the woman who was crippled in this biblical story for you.

Next, I invite you or your reflection group to create a cinquain that captures for you the righteous person in this biblical story. Finally, I invite you or your reflection group to create a cinquain that captures the character of Christ in this biblical story for you.

Now that you have finished creating these cinquains, I invite you or your reflection group to each share what you wrote about the woman in the biblical story who was crippled. What did you learn about infirmity or healing through the creation of your cinquain about her? What did you learn about her character through the cinquain that you created about her? What did you learn about her character from the cinquains that the other members of your group created?

I invite you or your reflection group to each share what you wrote about the character of the righteous person in this biblical story. What did you learn about righteousness through the creation of this cinquain? What did you learn about the character of this righteous person from the cinquain that you created? What did you learn about the character of the righteous person from the cinquains that the other members of your reflection group created?

Finally, I invite you or your reflection group to each share what you wrote about the character of Christ in this biblical story. What did you learn about the character of Christ from the cinquain that you created? What did you learn about the character of Christ from the cinquains that the other members of your reflection group created?

8. Healing of the Leper

(Mark 1:40–45)

And a leper came to him beseeching him, and kneeling said to him, "If you will, you can make me clean." Moved with pity, he stretched out his hand and touched him, and said to him, "I will; be clean." And immediately the leprosy left him, and he was made clean. And he sternly charged him, and sent him away at once, and said to him, "See that you say nothing to any one; but go, show yourself to the priest, and offer for your cleansing what Moses commanded, for a proof to the people." But he went out and began to talk freely about it, and to spread the news, so that Jesus could no longer openly enter a town, but was out in the country; and people came to him from every quarter.

If You Want To . . .

CAST

Leper	Man-1
Jesus	Man-2
Disciple	Coed-1
Righteous	Coed-2
Doctor	Coed-3
Mr. Jones	Bag Lady
Sister	Roomie-1
Boss	Roomie-2
Guest-1	Guest-3
Guest-2	

[**Note:** This drama is based on the miraculous healing of the leper which is found in Mark 1:40–45. After the gospel story has been proclaimed, three acting areas will be established. The center acting area will focus on the enactment of the biblical events. The acting areas on either side will deal with contemporary scenes from our society where we fracture rather than heal, where we isolate rather than incorporate into community.]

SCENE ONE

[*Jesus comes to the Center acting area accompanied by a disciple. There is also a righteous person at a distance who observes all the action and exchanges critically. Jesus is talking to the disciple when a*

163

leper comes up to him from the congregation. The leper is dressed in shabby attire. The leper wears very long pieces of colored yarn or material that characters from the following scenes will gradually attach to themselves as they move toward the congregation.]

LEPER:

(*The Leper slowly comes toward Jesus. The Disciple and Righteous Person are horrified. The Leper slowly kneels before Jesus and speaks.*)

If you want to, you can cure me. (*All the characters in the Center acting area freeze.*)

SCENE TWO

MAN-1:

Hey, would you take a look at that.

MAN-2:

Couldn't be from around here. She must be a transfer student.

MAN-1:

Well, the judges have just about tabulated their scorecards. And here are the results. (*Man-1 holds up a card reading "8.5" while Man-2 holds up a card reading "7.0."*)

Hey man, what are you, the Russian judge?

MAN-2:

No. I just don't believe in inflated scores. I don't want to ruin the scoring curve. Wait a minute. Do you see what I see?

MAN-1:

Oh my God, I've died and gone to heaven!

MAN-2:

Oh Venus, Venus de Milo . . .

MAN-1:

Control yourself long enough to vote.

MAN-2:

This takes no thought at all. (*Man-1 and Man-2 both hold up cards reading "10."*)

MAN-1:

At last we agree upon something. Oh-oh, I knew this was going to be too good to continue. (*Here Coed-1 walks in front of them near the congregation. She pauses.*)
      What do you call this?

MAN-2:

Visual pollution!

MAN-1:

How do you get to be like that?

MAN-2:

Visit Chernoble or eat too much Benson food!

MAN-1:

There ought to be a Campus Ordinance that people like her have to wear a bag over their head.

MAN-2:

Yeah! She's enough to upset the delicate ecological balance of the Mission Gardens. Are we ready to vote? (*Man-1 and Man-2 hold up cards reading "0" and "−1." Coed-1 slowly takes one of the Leper's pieces of colored yarn and puts it on her wrist. She moves toward the congregation and kneels in the same posture as the Leper, only facing and reaching out to the congregation. She freezes as the Leper in the Center area comes alive and speaks.*)

LEPER:

If you want to, you can cure me. (*The Leper freezes again.*)

SCENE THREE

[The Doctor in this scene is dressed in a white medical coat. The patient is dressed in a suit and tie.]

DOCTOR:

Mr. Jones, I got the results back and have had a chance to examine them.

JONES:

Well, Doctor, don't keep me in suspense. What's the verdict?

DOCTOR:

The test results were positive. I'm afraid that you do have AIDS.

JONES:

Oh my God! (*Long pause.*)
How much time do I have?

DOCTOR:

It's hard to say. In the past my experience has been that it takes anywhere from between six months and two years for a person's immune system to completely break down.

JONES:

But what do I do? Where do I go?

DOCTOR:

Mr. Jones, you don't go anywhere. My advice to you is to continue coming in for periodic check-ups. With many patients a great fear is communicating the disease to others. I can assure you that you cannot transmit this disease through any casual contact. (*The Doctor and Mr. Jones freeze. The Boss comes alive as he communicates the following information to Mr. Jones.*)

BOSS:

I really am sorry about this, Mark. I know what the Doctor said. The fact of the matter is, though, people around here are nervous. Even if you can't give it to them, you're at least contaminating the working environment. I'm sorry, Mark, but I'll have to let you go, for the good of us all. (*The Boss turns away from Mr. Jones. Mark then turns toward his Sister who has a baby buggy. He reaches out to her and she puts up an emphatic hand indicating "NO!" Mr. Jones then speaks to the Doctor.*)

JONES:

Doctor, what do I do? People are scared to death that I'm a disaster waiting to happen, a disease waiting to be transmitted. First I lose my job. Now my sister is afraid to come near me. She won't even let me see her new twins, my niece and nephew.

DOCTOR:

They're afraid, Mark. They fear what they don't know. Try and combat that ignorance with corrective information. I assure you, Mark, your disease simply cannot be communicated through any casual contact. I'd be happy to reassure your sister of this. (*The Doctor and Mr. Jones freeze while the Sister comes to life and speaks to her brother.*)

SISTER:

I know, Mark, I know I'm your sister. I know what the Doctor told you. I know you haven't seen the twins since they were born. But I'm scared, Mark. I'm their mother. What if the Doctor's wrong? I would never forgive you, that Doctor or myself. I know it hurts not to see them or me, Mark, but you've got to understand that I'm afraid. No, I don't want you to die, but I don't want my babies to die either. You've got to look at it from my position. (*The Sister freezes. Mr. Jones slowly comes alive and takes one of the pieces of colored yarn from the Leper and puts it on his wrist. Mr. Jones moves toward the congregation and kneels in the same position as the Leper.*

Mr. Jones faces and reaches out to the congregation as the Leper comes alive and speaks.)

LEPER:

If you want to, you can cure me. (*The Leper freezes again.*)

SCENE FOUR

[*During this scene a Bag Lady wanders in and begins poking through bags and looking through her treasures.*]

COED-3:

How was class?

COED-2:

Well, usually Political Economy is B-O-R-I-N-G! But today, for a change, it was superb!

COED-3:

What was so good about it?

COED-2:

We got onto a number of contemporary political and economic myths. The Professor absolutely demolished them.

COED-3:

Like what?

COED-2:

Like the myth that the poor are poor because of an unfair distribution of wealth; or the myth that the jobless rate is going up because of a decreasing number of jobs while the qualified work force is increasing; or the myth that the United States has a moral and ethical responsibility to share more of the earth's food with the world's hungry. (*By this time the Bag Lady is very visible. She is between the Coeds and the congregation.*)

COED-3:
Will you look at that!

COED-2:
Why does someone let herself disintegrate like that?

COED-3:
They have no pride, no healthy sense of self-worth.

COED-2:
How could someone like that live with herself?

COED-3:
She's probably squandered a good education that her family worked hard to provide for her.

COED-2:
I'll lay you odds she's wasted gobs of gifts and golden opportunities that she's had in life.

COED-3:
Doesn't she just make your hair friz? Don't you feel sorry for people like her?

COED-2:
Not at all! I agree with my Economics Professor. The poor and the unemployed are just looking for a handout. They're trying to make us feel guilty enough to give them a free ride. Well, they're not getting either from me!

COED-3:
Yeah, it would be un-American!

COED-2:
And un-Christian! God helps those who help themselves!

COED-3:
If people like her really wanted to eat or work, they could!

COED-2:

It's not that there's no food or jobs out there for the poor and the unemployed. The blathering idiots just don't know where to look for them! (*Coed-3 and Coed-2 freeze. The Bag Lady takes one of the pieces of colored yarn and puts it around her wrist. She takes the same kneeling posture as the Leper only she faces and reaches out to the congregation. The Leper then comes to life and speaks.*)

LEPER:

If you want to, you can cure me. (*The Leper freezes again.*)

SCENE FIVE

(*In this scene, both of the acting spaces, on either side of the biblical enactment, will be used. One space will be the Roommates' shared room. The other space will be a room where the party is being held.*)

ROOMIE-2:

What are you watching?

ROOMIE-1:

Tennis. It's the semi-finals of the French Open. (*The telephone rings. As Roomie-1 goes to answer it, he notices Roomie-2 working on something.*)
   Physics Lab, eh? (*Roomie-2 nods assent.*)
   Hey, Dude, I'm going to blow off a little steam and go to a party tonight. (*Roomie-1 gets ready and starts to leave. As he goes he casually speaks to Roomie-2.*)
   Later, Dude?

ROOMIE-2:

I'd love to go with you but the quarter is almost over and I really have to finish this Physics project. It counts for 75% of the grade.

ROOMIE-1:

> (*Roomie-2 freezes. Roomie-1 moves over to the other acting space. The people at the party come alive. Roomie-1 does a hand or arm gesture that Roomie-2 will imitate later. He does this gesture with his opening line.*) O.K. everybody, let's have a party! What have you got to drink for one thirsty hombre?

GUEST-1:

> Help yourself, John. What you don't see out can be found in the refrigerator.

GUEST-2:

> How about a brewski?

GUEST-3:

> How about a Lite? (*Guest-3 flicks on his thermal lighter.*)

ALL:

> No, a Bud Lite!

ROOMIE-1:

> I think I'll start with some of this Jack Daniels! Hey, Dude, it's so quiet in here that I think I'm at a wake. Crank up the portable ear drum demolisher! (*All the characters freeze. Roomie-2 comes alive again and closes his book. He wanders over into the party space. These people come alive again. No one pays any attention to him throughout this next part of the scene.*)

ROOMIE-2:

> O.K. everybody, let's have a party! (*Roomie-2 makes the same hand or arm gesture with this line that Roomie-1 did earlier.*) I heard the racket and thought I'd drop by to see what was happening. . . . If you don't mind, I'll grab something to drink. I'm kind of thirsty. . . . Does anybody know if there's some dietetic pop around here? . . . Well, I guess I better be getting back to that Physics project. It's a bear and it is 75% of the Quarter grade. . . . See you all later. (*Roomie-2 wanders back to his study room. He sits at the desk, opens a book and freezes.*)

GUEST-1:

Have any of you started that Physics project yet?

GUEST-2:

Why are you bringing that up? Do you want to ruin a perfectly good party?

GUEST-3:

Yeah! Do you want to bum us all out?

GUEST-1:

Well, no, but it does count for 75% of our Quarter grade, and I, for one, haven't done it!

ROOMIE-1:

Never fear, Johnnie's here! My roommate is a whiz at Physics. I'm sure "what's his name" would be happy to help us all out. He's got nothing better to do. This will at least give him some human contact. (*They all leave and go to Roomie-2's study space.*)

GUEST-1:

What's his name?

GUEST-2:

Quick, look on the door!

GUEST-3:

John.

ROOMIE-1:

I'm John, stupid. He must be Jim. (*They approach Roomie-2 with an obsequious manner.*)

Hey, Jim, buddy, old pal, got a minute?

ROOMIE-2:

Sure, guys. What's up? (*Here they all freeze for some moments. Then they burst out of the frozen position.*)

GUEST-1:

That wasn't so bad.

ROOMIE-1:

Yeah, but all this thinking has made me hungry. How about some pizza?

GUEST-2:

Sounds great!

ROOMIE-1:

Alright, we're out of here! Thanks a lot, eh . . . Dude. Later. (*Roomie-1, Guest-1, Guest-2 and Guest-3 all leave. Roomie-2 gets up and moves toward the Leper. Roomie-2 takes a piece of the colored yarn and puts it on his wrist. Roomie-2 then imitates the kneeling posture of the Leper. Roomie-2 faces and reaches toward the congregation as the Leper comes alive and speaks.*)

LEPER:

If you want to, you can cure me.

JESUS:

If I want to? Of course I want to. Be healed. (*Here Jesus reaches out and embraces the Leper. They freeze in a Tableau. If possible play John Michael Talbot's "St. Teresa's Prayer" from his* Song of the Shepherd *album. When this is finished the lights are dimmed and all the players return to places in the congregation.*)

Finis

PROPS

1. Six to eight long pieces of colored ribbon which are attached to the Leper's clothing when he comes on stage. The Coed, Mr. Jones, the Bag Lady and Roomie-2 each take one of

these and attach it to their wrist as they move out from the Leper to a different part of the congregation or audience.

2. Six Judging Cards with the following numbers printed on them:
   - (a) 8.5
   - (b) 7.0
   - (c) 10
   - (d) 10
   - (e) 0
   - (f) −1
3. One white medical coat for the Doctor.
4. One manila folder with assorted papers in it for the Doctor.
5. Four or five large plastic garbage bags with assorted odds and ends in them to represent the "treasures" of the Bag Lady.
6. One telephone.
7. Assorted books and papers for Roomie-2.
8. One thermal cigarette lighter. (An inexpensive Bic butane lighter with adjustable flame will do nicely.)
9. Assorted beer cans and liquor bottles filled with an appropriate colored water that approximates the color of the particular alcohol each contains.
10. One large portable radio/cassette player.

PRODUCTION NOTES

This biblical drama calls for nineteen players. And that number does not take into account the first two young women that Man-1 and Man-2 pass judgment on through their cards. Keep in mind that this biblical drama could be done with fewer players taking multiple parts.

This was originally performed as a dramatized homily at a Sunday evening student liturgy in the Santa Clara Mission Church. Although there are five scenes in the drama, we only did four. If you intend using it within a worship context, you might consider adapting its length in a similar manner.

Should you perform this drama in a non-liturgical context,

I strongly encourage you to read the biblical story from Mark's gospel (Mk 1:40–45) before you begin your performance. In this way the viewers can begin to make connections between the experience of the biblical story and the experience of the biblical drama.

When we performed this biblical drama in the Mission Church, we established three acting areas. The center acting area focused on the events of the biblical story. The players in this space would move in and out of tableaux. This means that at the appropriate times the players would act and speak. Then they would freeze (i.e., stand very still in their last position) until they were called upon to continue the action or dialogue. The acting areas on either side of this center area become the places where contemporary scenes from our society are enacted where we fracture rather than heal, where we isolate rather than incorporate into community.

The drama could be done as part of an educational event or adult Bible study group. If it is done this way, you could very profitably follow it up by using some of the reflection questions and exercises that I propose. After a few moments of silent reflection on what the group has just seen and heard, have the leader or facilitator of the reflection/study group begin by placing one of the following questions or exercises before the group for their consideration and response.

REFLECTION QUESTIONS AND EXERCISES

1. Every good story or drama has four main dramatic actions. They are: (a) the initiating action, (b) the developing action, (c) the climaxing action, and (d) the decisive action. I invite you or your reflection group to go through this story and focus on all the actions (verbs) in this biblical story. Try to identify what you think are the four "key words" or actions of this biblical story.

There will not always be agreement in a group about this. Don't allow this to be a stumbling block. When you have identified some of the key words or actions, begin exploring the contemporary and experiential significance of each word (action) for each member of your group. For instance, if one of your identified key words is "touched," consider what experiences and memories are locked inside of this word for your group. How do people in our society touch today? Why is physical abuse such a problem in our culture and society today? Why are there so many counseling centers for battered children and battered women? I will offer further suggestions for exploring the "healing" dimension of touch in another reflection question. This example, however, should give you an idea of how you or your reflection group can explore and uncover the experiences buried deep within each key word or action of the biblical story.

2. Walter Wink gave some sage advice to people exploring miracle stories from the scriptures in his book, *Transforming Bible Study* (Abingdon Press, 1980) when he said: "When I work with a miracle story, I follow Elizabeth Howes' advice and have the group list all the possibilities for accounting for the story, whether they believe them or not. . . . Now people are free to take their pick, but I never linger on the question, What *really* happened? because no one can know. We must acknowledge, in all honesty, that we cannot say what happened in these stories. . . . It is far more candid to list the possibilities and go right on to the question, Whatever happened, what does this story *mean*? than to pretend to know when we do not know" (p. 156).

In light of Wink's suggestion, I encourage you or your reflection group to imaginatively explore the following questions. In the Bible, leprosy was a general term for any kind of repulsive skin disease. It was not leprosy as we know it today (*New Jerome Biblical Commentary*). Who are some of the contemporary lepers of our society? Who are the untouchables in our world? Who are the untouchables in our country? Who are the untouchables in our state and city? Who are the untouchables in our school or dorm or classroom? Who are the untouchables in our church? Who or what made them untouchable?

Groups of people instinctively establish standards by which you are evaluated for inclusion (center of community) or exclusion (margins of community) in that society. Why do you or your reflection group think people do this? What kinds of community does this build? Are you part of any of these types of community? Why or why not? Who determines the standards? Is this fair? Is it fair to judge others by standards they have had no say in establishing? Why or why not? Explain. What are/should be the standards for inclusion in the authentic Christian community? Do the scriptures give us any clues as to what these standards might be? Make a list of all the ones you or your reflection group can think of together.

3. In your imagination, see yourself as the leper in this story. How do people treat you? How long have you been a leper? Was there a time in your life when you weren't a leper? How did your life change when you became a leper? What is most painful for you about being a leper? Is it lonely? Who are your friends? Who is your community? How did you hear about Jesus? Why do you go to him? What have you heard about Jesus? How do his disciples look at you and treat you? How does Jesus look at you and treat you? Why do you believe Jesus can help you? What does it feel like when Jesus reaches out and touches you? How do people treat you after your healing? How do you remember and treat those who were your community as a leper after you have been healed?

4. What does it mean in the biblical story when it says that Jesus "looked with pity" on the leper? Why do you or your reflection group think Jesus is so moved by the leper? What is it about the leper that touches Jesus so powerfully? Have you ever seen someone or experienced something that moved you deeply? What was there about the sight or the experience that moved you so much?

Gerard Manley Hopkins wrote a poem ("Spring and Fall") about a young girl watching a tree lose its leaves. She begins to cry. Hopkins poetically inquires whether she is actually grieving for the tree. He later concludes that this event for the tree somehow reminds the little girl about the preciousness of life and how she will one day give up her life as this tree gives up her leaves. She is, in the end, grieving for herself. This event of leaves falling from a tree gets her in touch with the inevitability of her own dying process. What do you or your reflection group think the leper touches in Jesus? Could the leper symbolize a part of Jesus or a way Jesus will be treated later in life? (Isaiah 53:1–6) What might the leper symbolize in you or the members of your reflection group?

5. I want you or your reflection group to consider the following questions about the biblical drama you either just finished reading or (preferably) seeing. It is important that each member of your reflection group listen to and respect the responses of the other members especially when they differ from your own.

In this biblical drama you saw the actions and heard the thoughts and sentiments of different characters. What did each one of you see? What did each of you hear? Did you like what you saw and heard? Why or why not? Explain. What struck you most about this biblical drama? Is this the way people really behave? Did the biblical drama exaggerate human attitudes and behaviors or did it truthfully present them? Would you want to change anything that the characters said or did in this biblical drama? What type of changes would you make? How would you go about making these changes?

6. What do you or your reflection group think about the attitudes and behaviors of the two young men in the second scene? Would you like to be judged strictly on appearances? Is this fair or unfair? Have you ever caught yourself doing this? Why or why not? Explain. Is this type of attitude and behavior helpful or hurtful? Explain.

What do you or your reflection group think about the attitudes and behaviors of the Doctor, the Boss and the Sister toward Mr. Jones in the third scene? If Mr. Jones were a relative, a classmate, a coworker of yours, what would your attitude and behavior toward him be? Would this attitude and behavior be supported or contradicted by Jesus' attitude and behavior toward the leper in the gospel story?

What do you or your reflection group think about the attitudes and behaviors of the two Coeds toward the Bag Lady in the fourth scene of this biblical drama? Would you or your reflection group agree or disagree with the reasoning and arguments of Coed-2 about the poor and the homeless? Explain. What attitudes do you or your reflection group think are behind the behaviors of the early Christian community mentioned in Acts 2:44–45? ("The faithful all lived together and owned everything in common; they sold their goods and possessions and shared out the proceeds among themselves according to what each one needed.") Explain. What attitudes do you or your reflection group think are behind the behaviors of the Christian community in 2 Corinthians 8:12–15? Explain.

What do you or your reflection group think about the attitudes and behaviors of the other characters toward Roomie-2 in the fifth scene of this biblical drama?

7. How was the leper in the biblical story cut off from his community? Why was he cut off from his community? How is a character in each scene of this biblical drama cut off from the community? Why are they cut off from the community? What attitudes and behaviors in ourselves, our culture, our church and our society cut people off from community instead of including them? When you or your reflection group identify some of these attitudes and behaviors, move on to consider how you might go about changing these attitudes and behaviors.

What does the Leper say to Jesus after each scene in the biblical dramatization? Why do the young woman, Mr. Jones, the Bag Lady and Roomie-2 all face the congregation/audience with arms outstretched when the Leper speaks to Jesus?

8. How does healing occur in the biblical story? What attitudes and behaviors of Jesus bring about healing for the leper? Have you ever experienced healing in your own life? How did healing happen for you? What characterized it? What specific qualities did it have? What people, what experiences, what actions have been healing for you in your life? Explain. Reflecting on how healing has come in your life may give you or your reflection group a few clues as to how healing came to the leper in the biblical story.

How might healing come to the different characters in this biblical dramatization? What shapes would healing take for the young woman in Scene Two, Mr. Jones in Scene Three, the

Bag Lady in Scene Four and Roomie-2 in Scene Five? Explain. Is standing with those in pain ultimately healing? Why or why not? Explain. Is mere presence healing? Why or why not? Explain. Does reaching out and touching (figuratively or literally) ultimately heal? Why or why not? Explain. How do you learn to carry the pain of another? Is this part of what it means to be a compassionate person? Why or why not? Explain. Have people helped you carry your pain in life? If so, how? If not, why not? Can sharing and listening to one another's stories of pain and joy, life and death, bring healing in community? Why or why not? Explain.

How did the leper affect Jesus? How was Jesus different after this encounter? We oftentimes imagine that the only person who is changed in these miracle stories is the person in need of healing. Couldn't Jesus discover something about his own heart and spirit through these encounters? Why or why not? Explain. What do you or your reflection group think Jesus discovers through this encounter with the leper?

How did the leper affect his community when he returned to them? Healing and health can challenge those parts of a system that are not healthy because it can call for change. Was the leper's community challenged? If so, how? If not, why not? Why do systems and groups (even diseased ones) instinctively resist change?

9. God Tests Abraham

(Genesis 22:1–19)

After these things God tested Abraham, and said to him, "Abraham!" And he said, "Here am I." He said, "Take your son, your only son Isaac, whom you love, and go to the land of Moriah, and offer him there as a burnt offering upon one of the mountains of which I shall tell you." So Abraham rose early in the morning, saddled his ass, and took two of his young men with him, and his son Isaac; and he cut the wood for the burnt offering, and arose and went to the place of which God had told him.

On the third day Abraham lifted up his eyes and saw the place afar off. Then Abraham said to his young men, "Stay here with the ass; I and the lad will go yonder and worship, and come again to you." And Abraham took the wood of the burnt offering, and laid it on Isaac his son; and he took in his hand the fire and the knife. So they went both of them together. And Isaac said to his father Abraham, "My father!" And he said, "Here am I, my son." He said, "Behold, the fire and the wood; but where is the lamb for a burnt offering?" Abraham said, "God will provide himself the lamb for a burnt offering, my son." So they went both of them together.

When they came to the place of which God had told him, Abraham built an altar there, and laid the wood in order, and bound Isaac his son, and laid him on the altar, upon the wood. Then Abraham put forth his hand, and took the knife to slay his son. But the angel of the LORD called to him from heaven, and said, "Abraham, Abraham!" And he said, "Here am I." He said, "Do not lay your hand on the lad or do anything to him; for now I know that you fear God, seeing you have not withheld your son, your only son, from me." And Abraham lifted up his eyes and looked, and behold, behind him was a ram, caught in a thicket by his horns; and Abraham went and took the ram, and offered it up as a burnt offering instead of his son. So Abraham called the name of that place The LORD will provide; as it is said to this day, "On the mount of the LORD it shall be provided."

And the angel of the LORD called to Abraham a second time from heaven, and said, "By myself I have sworn, says the LORD, because you have done this, and have not withheld your son, your only son, I will indeed bless you, and I will multiply your descendants as the stars of heaven and as the sand which is on the seashore. And your descendants shall possess the gate of their enemies, and by your descendants shall all the nations of the earth bless themselves, because you have obeyed my voice." So Abraham returned to his young men, and they arose and went together to Beer-sheba; and Abraham dwelt at Beer-sheba.

God Will Provide

CAST

Leader-1

Leader-2

Angel

SCU-1

SCU-2

SCU-3

Jennifer

C-M (Campus Minister)

Professor

Brian

Susan

Student-1

Student-2

Student-3

Ben

Mother

Carlotta

SCENE ONE

[*In this scene, different people come out of the congregation. They stand and read their statement from a piece of paper similar to the pieces of paper on which the students will have written down what community service they have done or will do as a lenten sacrifice. When each character is finished, they will go to an elevated bowl in the center with a charcoal fire in it. They will tear the paper in pieces and burn it. As they do that, the Angel will speak her lines.*]

LEADER-1:

(*He wears a U.N. flag.*) I am the leader of a country involved in war.

LEADER-2:

> (*He wears an Iraqi flag.*) I am the leader of a country involved in war. This is the place God has led me to.

LEADER-1:

> This is the place God has led me to. This is the place of sacrifice.

LEADER-2:

> This is the place of sacrifice. Our cause is just.

LEADER-1:

> Our cause is just. Our actions are holy.

LEADER-2:

> Our actions are holy. We are prepared to lay down our lives.

LEADER-1:

> We are prepared to lay down our lives. We shall drive our enemies from this place.

LEADER-2:

> We shall drive our enemies from this place, even if it means the spilling of blood.

LEADER-1:

> Even if it means the spilling of blood, with God on our side, victory is ours.

LEADER-2:

> With God on our side, victory is ours. (*Leader-1 and Leader-2 move to the elevated bowl in the center. They rip up their pieces of paper and watch them burn as the Angel comes to position behind the bowl and speaks.*)

ANGEL:

> Is this the sacrifice God asks of you? (*Leader-1 and Leader-2 go sit in the congregation. Angel moves back. SCU-1 comes out from the congregation.*)

SCU-1:

I am a young person. This is the place God has led me to. This is the place of sacrifice. My life is a constant struggle with questions about my family, my identity, intimacy and relationships. (*SCU-1 goes to the elevated bowl and tears her paper into pieces and then burns it. As she does this the Angel moves forward and speaks.*)

ANGEL:

Is this the sacrifice God asks of you? (*Angel moves back. SCU-1 goes and sits in the congregation as SCU-2 comes into the acting area.*)

SCU-2:

I am a friend and classmate of Rob Hayes. This is the place God has led me to. This is the place of sacrifice. I am confused. I am frightened. I am angry and hurting. Rob was so young. He had his whole life in front of him. I want to believe there is a God but how does a loving God allow such things to happen? (*SCU-2 goes to the elevated bowl. She tears her paper into pieces and burns them. The Angel moves forward and speaks.*)

ANGEL:

Is this the sacrifice God asks of you? (*Angel moves back. SCU-2 goes and sits in the congregation. SCU-3 comes into the acting area.*)

SCU-3:

I am a student at Santa Clara University. This is the place God has led me to. This is the place of sacrifice. In many ways my life is comfortable. I am removed from the physical pain of a world at war. I wrestle with how to achieve my own ideals without giving up my respect and sensitivity to the needs of others. (*SCU-3 goes to the elevated bowl. She tears her paper into pieces and burns them. The Angel moves forward and speaks.*)

ANGEL:

Is this the sacrifice God asks of you? (*SCU-3 goes and sits in the congregation.*)

Why do you waste your time and energy worrying? Surely you must know . . .

ALL:

God will provide. (*Angel leaves the acting area as the lights dim. After a few moments of silence the lights come up on Scene Two.*)

SCENE TWO

[*In this scene the character who plays the Spirit inspires the characters who encounter Jennifer to speak to her about topics other than the expected or anticipated agenda. These characters are never consciously aware of the presence of the Spirit in the room.*]

JENNIFER:

(*She is studying one of her books in a distracted and half-hearted manner when her mother comes in .*) Sighhhhh.

SPIRIT:

It's awful quiet in there. Why not look in on Jen.

MOTHER:

It's awful quiet in here. What's up, Jen?

JENNIFER:

Oh God, I have sooo much homework!

SPIRIT:

What's really bothering her?

MOTHER:

I think I recognize this pattern. Jen, what's really bothering you?

JENNIFER:

I'm just really stressed out. I really can't understand anything I'm reading about research methods.

SPIRIT:

She's working too hard.

MOTHER:

This may sound strange for a mother to say but I really think you're working too hard.

JENNIFER:

Well, I have an exam coming up and I really need to know what I'm doing.

SPIRIT:

She doesn't really have her heart in psychology.

MOTHER:

Why don't you do something you can put your heart into, something you really enjoy rather than something you think you have to do, like psychology?

JENNIFER:

If you and Dad taught me anything it was to honor commitments even when it involves some frustration and hard work.

SPIRIT:

That she's happy is more important to you than what her major is.

MOTHER:

Your father and I don't care what you study, Jen, or what your major is. What we want more than anything is that you are happy. And right now you don't sound or look very happy. (*Jennifer and Mother freeze. The Spirit moves over to the Campus Minister's office. Jennifer walks over to the area of the stage where the Campus Minister is and sits down.*)

JENNIFER:
So how did I do in my evaluation?

SPIRIT:
You don't want to talk about the evaluation.

C-M:
Jen, you did fine. But I don't want to talk about your student evaluation.

SPIRIT:
What's she doing?

C-M:
I want to talk about what you're doing.

SPIRIT:
Why's she studying psychology?

C-M:
I hope this won't sound presumptuous of me but I have to ask it. Why are you studying psychology?

SPIRIT:
She went to a performing arts high school.

C-M:
Didn't you tell me you went to a performing arts high school?

JENNIFER:
Well, yes.

SPIRIT:
She liked it, too.

C-M:
And didn't you tell me you really enjoyed it?

JENNIFER:

Yes, I did.

SPIRIT:

Then why doesn't she major in something she likes.

C-M:

Then why aren't you majoring in something you enjoy, like Theater Arts?

JENNIFER:

I really do like it, but I thought it might be taking the easy way out.

SPIRIT:

God didn't create her to be miserable.

C-M:

Jen, there's nothing holy about being miserable.

SPIRIT:

She's got to trust her instincts and listen to her heart.

C-M:

Your talents, your desires, your heart are God-given gifts. Trust them. Listen to them. (*Jennifer and the Campus Minister freeze. The Spirit moves over to Carlotta. Jennifer then makes her way over to where Carlotta is standing.*)

SPIRIT:

She looks preoccupied.

CARLOTTA:

Earth to Jen. Come in please.

JENNIFER:

Oh, hi Carlotta. I almost didn't see you. I'm a bit distracted these days.

SPIRIT:
  What about?

CARLOTTA:
  What about?

SPIRIT:
  Tell her, she'll understand.

JENNIFER:
  I'm thinking about changing my major and transferring to another college.

SPIRIT:
  What is she trying to find?

CARLOTTA:
  What are you looking for, Jen?

SPIRIT:
  Trust her. She'll understand.

JENNIFER:
  I know a lot of people would think I'm crazy or a religious kook, but I think you'll understand. I want to go to a school that has more of a Christian atmosphere.

SPIRIT:
  Go on.

JENNIFER:
  I'd like to live in a place where Campus Ministry was an important part of dorm life.

SPIRIT:
  Keep going.

JENNIFER:
  I'd like to be part of a faith community where the students took an active part in the liturgies.

SPIRIT:

What about words and actions.

JENNIFER:

I'd like to go somewhere where the words "faith" and "justice" were not just nice rhetoric but experiences that students wrestled with in their everyday life.

SPIRIT:

What about your nephew?

CARLOTTA:

You know something, Jen, I have a nephew who went to a small liberal arts university up north.

SPIRIT:

Jesuit philosophy.

CARLOTTA:

While I'm sure they don't succeed with every student that goes there, they challenge their students to become "men and women for others." And I'm happy to say they succeeded with my nephew.

SPIRIT:

Don't forget the theater program.

CARLOTTA:

It also seems to me that I have heard they have a very good theater program. You ought to investigate it, Jen. (*Jennifer and Carlotta freeze. The Spirit moves over by Mark. Jennifer then gets up and goes over to Mark.*)

JENNIFER:

Excuse me. Are you Professor Lang?

MARK:

Why yes, I am. You must be Jennifer. The secretary said you wanted to see me.

SPIRIT:

Maybe you can help.

MARK:

How can I be of assistance to you?

JENNIFER:

I was thinking of transferring schools and going into a Theater Arts major. Since you know that field pretty well, I was wondering if you could make any suggestions.

SPIRIT:

What about the two new bulletins?

MARK:

What a coincidence! Today I received two University bulletins in the mail. They both have fine Theater programs. You might like to try this one. (*Mark starts to hand her a bulletin.*)

SPIRIT:

The other one might be better.

MARK:

(*Pulls the first bulletin back.*) You know something, Jen. It's just a hunch, but I think you might be happier with the program at this school. (*Mark hands Jennifer the Santa Clara University bulletin.*)

SPIRIT:

You know some of the professors there.

MARK:

I know a few of the professors there and I think you'd learn a lot from them.

SPIRIT:

You know some students who graduated.

MARK:

> I also know a few of the graduates of their program and they spoke very highly about it.

JENNIFER:

> (*She takes the bulletin.*) Thanks, Professor Lang. I appreciate all the help. I'll look this over and give the school and its program some serious thought. (*All characters freeze.*)

SPIRIT:

> Why are you afraid? Why do you waste your time and energy worrying? Surely you must know that . . .

ALL:

> God will provide. (*The lights dim as everyone in Scene Two returns to the congregation. Brian and Ben set themselves for Scene Three and the lights come up.*)

SCENE THREE

[*As this scene opens, Brian is straightening up his room. Bro. Ben, the Resident Minister, comes by and knocks on the door.*]

BEN:
> Anybody home?

BRIAN:
> Oh, Bro. Ben, come on in. I'm just trying to straighten this mess of a room up.

BEN:
> I haven't seen you in a while. How have you been?

BRIAN:
> Busy. Too busy!

BEN:

Why's that?

BRIAN:

I don't really know. All I know is that I'm not doing a very good job of juggling all the things I have to do. Trying to be an RA, a student, a senior, a boyfriend, a Christian, a human being, a "fill-in-the-blank," is just more than I can handle at times.

BEN:

Sounds like you need a couple more hands to juggle all of this.

BRIAN:

Actually, I'm glad you came by, Ben. I feel bad that I've been running around like a chicken with its head cut off. Lent has already started and I haven't even thought of anything I can sacrifice or do to make the season special.

BEN:

Given your present condition I think there might be a spiritual hernia in the making if you took too much more on. I would look for something simple or some way of simplifying your life.

BRIAN:

Sure doesn't sound like much, Ben.

BEN:

Little things are little things. But faithfulness in little things is a great thing. Well, I'll love ya and leave ya, Brian, but remember: go gently and be good to yourself. (*Ben leaves.*)

BRIAN:

Later, Ben. (*Brian continues moving things around and straightening things up as Susan walks in.*)

SUSAN:

Is this a Dead Head I see before my eyes?

BRIAN:

Oh, Susan, are you a life-saver.

SUSAN:

What's this? Are we drowning? Are we sending out an S.O.S.?

BRIAN:

I am exhausted. My Day Calendar is filled. I've got no time for myself. I really need to get out of Swig for a night. I've been looking forward to this Dead Head Concert with you for weeks. Let's get out of here before the roof falls in. O.K.?

SUSAN:

I am ready and willing. Maestro, a little traveling music! (*Just as they are about to leave, Student-1 knocks at the door.*)

STUDENT-1:

Brian, I'm supposed to have this registration form for classes in by tomorrow and I don't have any idea what to take or how to fill it out.

SUSAN:

I'll wait outside.

BRIAN:

Well, Krista, slow down and take it easy. Why not take a deep breath. (*Krista takes in a deep breath but holds it.*)

Good. It's also good to let go of that breath, Krista. Just look upon breathing as borrowing that air temporarily. Not stockpiling it. The first thing you need to do is get a No. 2 pencil.

STUDENT-1:

O.K. I've got one of those. But I don't even know what teachers to ask for.

BRIAN:

Well, I'll look at your class schedule here and see what we have to choose from. Now this teacher would be good. I've taken her class. I've heard this teacher is very challenging and good from friends of mine. But this one . . . well, I'd stay away from his class.

STUDENT-1:

Really?

BRIAN:

Yeah. (*Together with Krista.*)
Moynahan.

STUDENT-1:

I've heard about his class.

BRIAN:

Yeah, steer clear of him.

STUDENT-1:

But where do I turn this in?

BRIAN:

Over at Walsh Administration building. (*Krista has a blank look.*)

It's right across from the De Saisset Art Gallery. So, are you alright now?

STUDENT-1:

Yeah. I feel much better. I better go get this thing filled out now. See you later, Brian. Thanks for all the help.

BRIAN:

O.K., Krista, see you later. (*Susan comes back in.*)

Whew. Let's get out of here. Gerry Garcia is waiting for us. (*Susan and Brian start to go when Student-2 knocks on the door.*)

STUDENT-2:

Brian, I'm really sorry to be bothering you right now but I really need your help.

BRIAN:

Well, Susan and I were just on our way out. Do you think it could wait till tomorrow?

STUDENT-2:

It could, but there might not be a Swig building still here in the morning.

BRIAN:

What's the matter.

STUDENT-2:

Well, it's like this. I plugged in my curling iron two hours ago. I got a long distance phone call and forgot all about it. I went down the hall to check out what was happening and when I just came back my room was filled with smoke.

BRIAN:

That's funny, I didn't hear any smoke alarm go off.

STUDENT-2:

(*Somewhat embarrassed.*) Well, I took out the battery and used it on my electric eyebrow plucker.

BRIAN:

Susan, sorry. I'll be right back. I better check this out.

SUSAN:

No problem. (*Brian and Student-2 take a few steps off the platform and freeze. Someone comes onto the acting area with a sign that reads* TIME PASSES. *When the sign has been shown to all and removed, Brian returns to the main platform while Student-2 goes back to the congregation.*)

BRIAN:

    Oh, Susan, I'm really sorry. I know this will make us a little late, but at least we'll catch most of the concert. Let me get my jacket and we'll be out of here. (*As Brian goes to get his jacket Student-3 knocks on the door.*)

STUDENT-3:

    Dude, I'm really sorry to bother you but my roommate is in the bathroom throwing up his guts. His eyes are all purple or something.

BRIAN:

    Sounds like he's had too much to drink again.

STUDENT-3:

    I think it's really bad this time because he's spitting up blood too. He's really messed up, Brian. He won't stop retching and I'm afraid he's going to pass out. I don't know what to do. Would you come and take a look?

BRIAN:

    Susan, what can I say?

SUSAN:

    Nothing. Just hurry. You may have to call "911."

STUDENT-3:

    Must be a major fine if your roommate dies, huh? We never should have drunk that lighter fluid. (*Brian and Student-3 move off the acting platform and freeze. Someone comes on with a placard that reads* MORE TIME PASSES. *After everyone has seen the placard, it is removed. Brian comes back to the acting area and Student-3 goes back to the congregation.*)

BRIAN:

    Oh, Susan, what time is it? One-thirty in the morning. I'm sorry we missed the concert.

SUSAN:

There was nothing you could do about that, Brian. It's getting late. I'm sure you could use some rest and I know that I could. I guess I'll see you tomorrow?

BRIAN:

I'll make this up to you, Susan, I promise you.

SUSAN:

That's O.K. . . . . (*As Susan is leaving, Bro. Ben comes in.*)

BEN:

I hear you went to a concert tonight. I was glad to hear you did something nice for yourself.

BRIAN:

Well, I intended to go to a concert but we had a few unexpected emergencies.

BEN:

Everything O.K.?

BRIAN:

Yeah. I'll give you a blow-by-blow description tomorrow. Maybe you could give me some ideas about what we talked about earlier this evening. You know, something I can sacrifice or do for Lent.

BEN:

Maybe you don't have to find something to give up or sacrifice. Maybe that will find you. For myself I just try to listen and be open to what God asks of me each day. And it's always new and unexpected. So, Brian, get some rest and we'll talk some more in the morning. (*Ben and Brian freeze. The Angel comes on stage and speaks.*)

ANGEL:
Why do you waste your time and energy worrying? Surely you must know that . . .

ALL:
God will provide.

Finis

PROPS

1. Five pieces of colored paper that characters in Scene One can write on.
2. One small United Nations flag worn by Leader-1 on his coat.
3. One small Iraqi flag worn by Leader-2 on his coat.
4. One incense bowl on a stand.
5. One book that Jennifer uses in Scene Two.
6. Four bar stools to be used in Scene Two and Scene Three.
7. One black clerical shirt and white collar to be worn by the Campus Minister in Scene Two.
8. Two college bulletins for use in Scene Two.
9. One piece of paper to serve as a "Registration Form" in Scene Three.
10. One number two pencil to be used by Student-1 in Scene Three.
11. One class schedule for use in Scene Three.
12. One placard with the words TIME PASSES printed on it for Scene Three.
13. One placard with the words MORE TIME PASSES printed on it for Scene Three.

PRODUCTION NOTES

This biblical dramatization was created and performed as a dramatized homily at a Mission Church liturgy on the second Sunday in Lent, 1991. It was part of a Lenten Series entitled

"Becoming A Community of Compassion" that was sponsored by Campus Ministry at Santa Clara University.

The Biblical Explorers decided to work with this passage from the Old Testament for a number of reasons. Three years earlier we had worked with the gospel selection for this Sunday in Lent. While we were confident that our understanding and dramatic interpretation of the transformation would have been different from our previous effort (see *What On Earth Does It Mean?* in this collection of story dramas), the group thought it would be good to work with this powerful passage from the Old Testament that dealt with the sacrifice of Isaac.

The notion of "sacrifice" was central to the faith community's celebration of Lent this year. The Campus Ministry staff, who regularly organize the University Community's celebrations of the liturgical seasons, saw "sacrifice" as an essential ingredient to our gradually becoming a community whose care is expressed in compassionate action.

This particular year, the congregation was invited to give expression to their sacrifices which attempted to embody the traditional lenten observances of prayer, fasting and almsgiving. The previous Sunday the congregation had been invited to spend some time in volunteer work. The colored pieces of paper were given out to everyone as they entered the mission. Just after the Prayers of the Faithful and prior to the Preparatory Rite, the congregation was asked to write down the service they had actually done or would do in the coming week. These were collected and brought up with the other gifts of bread and wine. This explains why colored pieces of paper are used in Scene One. This also may be a place where, if you are not doing something similar in your own church, you may wish to adapt this biblical dramatization for your own needs and purposes.

It is very important that in Scene Two the characters not visually acknowledge the character "Spirit." The other characters in this scene act as if Spirit is not even in the room. In this way, they will communicate that the character which the congregation can see and hear cannot be seen by the other characters in Scene Two. Spirit is constantly suggesting things to the characters. Spirit suggest thoughts that find verbal expression in these other characters' mouths.

There is an old dictum in the theater that you should always work with your props and costumes ahead of time to make sure that they work. I did not do that with the elevated bowl with the charcoal fire that is called for in Scene One. This prop was hastily adapted (i.e., a candle in a tinfoil wrapped bowl) shortly before the liturgy. As pieces of paper were burned in it, the candle wax began to heat up and a small fire resulted. It almost became an insurmountable distraction for the rest of the liturgy until I requested that the bowl and fire be removed. None of this needed to occur had we practiced with this prop ahead of time. A word to the wise should be sufficient.

The world event that provided the background for Scene One was the mounting hostilities in the Persian Gulf. The flags that Leader-1 and Leader-2 wore represented the opposing factions. The rhetoric used in this scene by the two characters is frighteningly close to that used by actual participants. The words of Bob Dylan's war ballad, "With God On Our Side," in light of this recent Gulf conflict, are as hauntingly true today as they were during the Vietnam War. The scene challenges all parties to take a good hard look at the attitudes behind their behavior. It asks a difficult but essential question we can repeatedly ask about the decisions we make in our life: "Is this the sacrifice God asks of you?"

Some of the terminology in Scene Three may be a bit baffling. An "RA" is a Resident Assistant. This is a Junior or Senior year University student who lives on the floor of a Residence Hall as a resource person, peer counselor and representative of university policy. This is an important service position that greatly affects the student's experience of residence life.

REFLECTION QUESTIONS AND EXERCISES

1. This powerful and beautiful story from the Old Testament (Gen 22:1–19) narrates the tenth and greatest trial of Abraham (*New Jerome Biblical Commentary*). Scripture scholars generally agree that in the Abraham stories he experiences ten trials and seven blessings.

I invite you or your reflection group to consider the ways that you, like Abraham, have been "put to the test." What have been some of the more "trying" moments and experiences of your life? Why not spend some moments going over your life and jotting down in your journal the moments and experiences that suggest themselves to you. If possible, share some of these with the other members of your reflection group.

When asked by Isaac what they shall sacrifice, Abraham responds: "God will provide." What do you think Abraham meant by this? Have you or your reflection group ever experienced the truth of Abraham's words: "God will provide"? Have you ever experienced this during those "trying" moments and experiences of your life? Why or why not? Explain.

Abraham not only experiences God testing him but blessing him as well. I invite you or your reflection group to spend some time looking back over your life and considering the different ways God may have blessed you. Jot down in your journal whatever suggests itself to you as you are reflecting on God's blessings in your life. If possible, share some of these blessings with the other members of your reflection group. In this way, we remind people of other blessings in their lives.

2. I invite you or the members of your reflection group to enter into this biblical story in some imaginative ways that were suggested by the work of Professor Doug Adams who is a founding member of The Center for the Arts in Religion and Education.

First of all, imagine that you are Abraham. God has just spoken to you and told you to sacrifice your beloved Isaac. What are you thinking, feeling or physically sensing? Give a word to what you are thinking, feeling or physically sensing. Now give physical and facial expression to this feeling and this word. Become a statue of response.

Second, imagine that you are Isaac. Your father, Abraham, whom you love and trust, had told you earlier that God would provide the sacrifice. You have watched your father build the altar and arrange the wood. Then he takes you and binds your hands and feet and puts you on the altar. Your father stretches out his hand with a knife to kill you. What are you thinking, feeling or physically sensing? Put that thought, feeling or physical sensation in a word. Now give physical and facial expression to that word. Become a statue of response.

Third, imagine that you are Abraham. Your child, Isaac, has asked you what you are going to sacrifice and you have told him: "God will provide." You have built the altar and arranged the wood. Now you take your child and bind his hands and feet. You place him on the altar. You pick up the knife and stretch out your hand to sacrifice him as God has commanded you. At that moment, what are you thinking, feeling or physically sensing? Put that thought, feeling or physical sensation in a word. Now give physical and facial expression to that word. Become a statue of response.

Fourth, you are Abraham. Just as you are about to fulfill God's command, an Angel holds your hand and restrains you. God sees your faithfulness and readiness to give up what is most precious in your eyes. God doesn't wish you to harm Isaac. Instead, you are to offer a nearby ram in sacrifice. Because of your obedience, God will bless you and your descendants forever. At this moment, what are you thinking, feeling or physically sensing. Put that thought, feeling or physical sensation into a word. Give physical and facial expression to that word. Become a statue of response.

Fifth, you are Isaac. Do you, too, hear the Angel's voice? When the Angel speaks and you hear that your life will be spared, what are you thinking, feeling or physically sensing? Put that thought, feeling or physical sensation into a word. Now give physical and facial expression to that word. Become a statue of response.

It would also be quite challenging and educational to do this same exercise from the perspective of God. What do you or your reflection group think God might be thinking, feeling or sensing at these different moments? Put those thoughts, feelings or physical sensations into a word. Give those words physical and facial expression. Become a statue of response from God's perspective.

As a result of these exercises, what do you or your reflection group learn about the character, Abraham? What do you learn about the character, Isaac? What do you learn about God in this story? When Sarah finds out what took place on that mountain, what do you imagine would be her thoughts, feelings or physical sensations? Put one of those thoughts, feelings or physical sensations into a word. Now give physical and facial expression to those words. Become statues of response from Sarah's perspective.

3. In a video program entitled "Exploring Biblical Humor" which I made for Tabor Publishing in 1991 (for further information contact: Tabor Publishing, One DLM Park, Allen, Texas 75002. Toll Free Telephone Number: 1-800-527-4747.), I suggest two creative dramatic tools that you or your reflection group can use to further explore the riches of this biblical story.

First of all, have the members of your reflection group act out this biblical story as a "narrative mime." Each member of the reflection group becomes a character in the story (e.g., Abraham, Isaac, Angel, Servant, etc.). One person acts as a narrator. As the narrator slowly reads the story, the members of the reflection group perform the actions of their character. After you have gone through the story in this way, move on to use the second suggested creative dramatic tool.

The next creative dramatic tool that you can use builds upon the experience of the narrative mime. The first time that I saw it used was by a colleague of mine, Norm Fedder, from Kansas State University. He did not use it in conjunction with the Narrative Mime technique.

This second creative dramatic technique is the Interview Show along the lines of Phil Donahue. Your guests are the characters from this story. Be sure to include Sarah so you can get her reactions to all of this. The host interviews each character and can explore what they were thinking, feeling and physically sensing in this biblical story. To assist you in this, have the reflection group brainstorm on what questions they would like to ask these characters that will help reveal their attitudes, their behaviors and their faith. Be sure and allow, as most interview shows do, questions from the audience. What this technique calls for is imaginative identification. We don't know what Abraham or Isaac or Sarah were thinking or feeling or physically sensing. But we can know what we might think or feel or sense in a similar situation and this gives us clues and insight into the biblical characters and the biblical story.

4. In the second scene of the biblical dramatization, the Campus Minister says to Jennifer: "There's nothing holy about being miserable." What do you or your reflection group think about this evaluation? Do you agree or disagree? Explain. Do you think there is truth or wisdom in the Campus Minister's words? Why or why not? Explain.

St. Ignatius of Loyola, in *The Spiritual Exercises,* talks about what pleases God in his first consideration entitled "The First Principle and Foundation" (No. 23). In it, he says that men and women were created "to praise, reverence and serve God."

What do you or your reflection group understand the word "praise" to mean? What are some of the different shapes and expressions that your "praise" takes?

What do you or your reflection group understand the word "reverence" to mean? What are some of the different shapes and expressions that your "reverence" takes?

What do you or your reflection group understand the word "serve" to mean? What are some of the different shapes and expressions that "service" can take?

Do you or your reflection group agree or disagree with St. Ignatius' understanding of what men and women are here on this earth to do? Explain.

5. In Scene Three of the biblical dramatization, Brian tells Brother Ben that he has been "running around like a chicken with its head cut off." Have you ever felt that you were living your life the way the character Brian describes his? Do you ever feel that you have too many "hats" to wear or "tasks" to juggle?

The character Ben suggests to Brian that an appropriate way to enter into the spirit of Lent might be by looking for some way of simplifying his life. What are some of the ways you think you could live your life more simply? Come up with as many examples as you can. Explore the significance and implications of simplifying your life in each of these ways.

6. In Scene Three of the biblical dramatization, Brother Ben says to Brian: "Little things are little things. But faithfulness in little things is a great thing." What do you or your reflection group think of this evaluation? Would you agree or disagree? Explain. Do you find any truth or wisdom in Brother Ben's words? Why or why not? Explain.

What are some of the "little things" in your life? What shapes or expressions would "faithfulness" in these "little things" take in your life? How can you be faithful in the little things of your life?

7. What do you or your reflection group understand by the term "physical exercises"? What is the goal of physical exercise? What happens when a person stops doing any form of physical exercise?

Why do you think St. Ignatius of Loyola titled his work *The Spiritual Exercises*? What do you or your reflection group understand by the term "spiritual exercises"? What do you think is the goal of spiritual exercises? What happens to a person when they stop doing any form of spiritual exercise?

What do you or your reflection group think is the purpose of the Christian observance of Lent? What are we preparing for through our lenten observance? The gospel from the mass for Ash Wednesday suggests three spiritual exercises that Christians have traditionally used to enter more fully into the spirit and experience of Lent. Those three spiritual exercises are: prayer, fasting and almsgiving. What do you or your reflection group understand by the terms "prayer," "fasting," and "almsgiving"? What are some of the different shapes and expressions that these traditional spiritual exercises might take in our culture and society today?

8. I invite you or your reflection group to create a cinquain (i.e., a five-line piece of poetry) on "sacrifice" and then another cinquain on "holiness." Remember that the first line consists of the word that is the subject or title of your poetic reflection (i.e., either "sacrifice" or "holiness"). The second line consists of two descriptive adjectives that capture or convey your subject. The

third line consists of three participles (i.e., action words, verbs ending in "ing") that capture active dimensions of your first-line subject. The fourth line consists of a four-word descriptive phrase that summarizes your subject. The fifth line consists in a one-word restatement of your first-line subject. The final line/word usually brings out some nuanced dimension of the first line/word and is an emphatic or gentle restatement of it.

When you have finished creating these cinquains, share them with the other members of your reflection group. What do you discover about "sacrifice" through the creation and sharing of these cinquains? What do you discover about "holiness" through the creation and sharing of these cinquains?